PIERO TORR

Former Superintendent Artistic a
of the Provinces of Siena a

Orvieto

Complete guide to the city

···▸ **The churches**

···▸ **The museums**

···▸ **The palazzi**

···▸ **The Etruscan necropoli**

···▸ **The city underground**

···▸ **Folklore**

···▸ **The environs**

···▸ **Plan of the city**

···▸ **Useful information**

BONECHI EDIZIONI "IL TURISMO"

*O*rvieto began its journey on the long road to civilization in protohistory, with the primitive protovillanovan and Villanovan peoples who settled here between the 12th and 8th-7th centuries B.C. It was the Etruscans, though, who established a permanent and important settlement on top of and around the base of this tufa plateau, between 15 and 60 meters high over the valley of the River Paglia. The cliff, like others in the valley, owes its origins to the so-called "Volsinii Volcanoes" with four craters which erupted and blocked an inlet of the Tyrrhennian Sea that at the time lapped the foothills of Città della Pieve and where the Tiber had its outlet. The waters of this gulf or inlet gradually disappeared and the area turned into a fertile plain.

After the Etruscans, the conquering Romans wiped out the city in 264 B.C., and carried off an enormous amount of plunder to Rome, while the inhabitants were deported to the Lake of Bolsena.

In the early Middle Ages Orvieto was once more subject to bar-

barian invasions, above all by Totila and Agilulfo, and eventually became a free Commune. But the bitter fratricidal struggles between Guelphs and Ghibellines – especially between the Monaldeschi and the Filippeschi – brought various local families to power, first one then the other. Around 1354 Cardinal Egidio Albornoz, in the service of the Church, arrived in Orvieto, and ordered an imposing fortress to be built for defense. Even so, it was not until around 1450, after harsh rebellions, that the entire territory fell under the rule of

▲▼ Views of the medieval city

► Fortezza Albornoz, entrance gate

papal Rome, until the Unification of Italy.

Despite all this, civilization in Orvieto continued with its ups and downs up to the present day, with outstanding examples of Italian art and culture in almost every century. The fame of Orvieto depends not so much on the fact that it was an Etruscan city and that a host of urban structures still bears witness to the later Romanesque, Gothic and Renaissance periods but first and foremost Orvieto is famous for its Cathedral, one of the most noble and splendid buildings of Romanesque/Gothic art in Europe[1].

(1) A precious source for historical and artistic information on Orvieto is the small book by Pericle Perali ("Orvieto", publ. 1919) which all later writers on the city have referred to, well aware of certain understandable inaccuracies.

► The city up high on the cliff can be reached by road, or via a cable car (funicolare) which leaves across from the railroad station or via elevators and escalators that take you from a large covered parking area known as "Campo della Fiera" to the historical center, near the church of San Giovanni.

The Cathedral and the Museums on the Square

Once you have "landed" on top of the cliff, your visit of Orvieto and its art and monuments can begin with the cathedral. A walk through the dark medieval streets and alleys will suddenly and unexpectedly bring you to a light-filled square where a glittering enchanted vision seems to rise up skywards. Before building of this new great church began in 1290, on the foundations of an Etruscan temple, the older cathedral of Santa Maria and the small church of San Costanzo already on this site had to be torn down. As early as 1199, with Santa Maria falling into ruin, the clergy had to hold their services in other churches in the city. It was at this time that the Orvietani and the clergy had broached the idea of building a new cathedral. Ostensibly however, the people of Orvieto and Pope Nicholas IV, who blessed the foundation stone, had this new great church built to house the fragments of the consecrated host and the famous linen altar cloth stained with blood in the miracle of Bolsena of 1263. These miraculous relics had immediately been brought to Orvieto and on August 11th of the following year (1264) Pope Urban IV had instituted the solemn church feast of Corpus Christi.

Fra Bevignate da Gubbio (the famous builder, together with Nicola and Giovanni Pisano, of the Fontana Maggiore in Perugia) must have been the first *capomastro* in charge of building the cathedral, most probably designed by the even more famous Arnolfo di Cambio, Florentine sculptor and architect subsequently of, among others, the Cathedral of Florence. The church was begun as Romanesque, in basilica form with a nave and two side aisles, which became Gothic as time passed, with the typical cross vaulting in the apse by Giovanni di Uguccione, who succeeded Fra Bevignate. In the early 1300s (c 1308) the Sienese sculptor and architect, Lorenzo Maitani "universalis caput magister" was called in because several faults had appeared in the structure of the external walls. Maitani reinforced them with strong flying buttresses which can still be seen and within which two chapels were later set, the Cappella del Corporale on the right and that of San Brizio on the left. He then enlarged, and by this time in purely Gothic style, the transept with the square apse (the original semicircular one was torn down), into the center of which the great four-light window was set, later (1328-34) decorated with stained glass by master Giovanni di Bonino. Around 1310 he also began work on the sublime facade which looks like an immense precious reliquary, divided into three parts corresponding to the nave and two side aisles, by four great piers terminating in spires. The

▶ Facade of the Cathedral
designed by Lorenzo Maitani (1310-1330)

tallest spire, on the right, was not raised until 1503 by Michele Sanmicheli, and was then finished by Antonio da Sangallo the Younger. It was later struck by lightning and was rebuilt in 1795 by Giuseppe Valadier.

The numerous architects/*capomastri* who followed Maitani on the whole returned to this master's original plans. At least one of the two drawings on parchment still extant (Museo dell'Opera) is given to Maitani. These famous *capomastri* from Pisa, Siena and Florence included Andrea Pisano (1347) and Andrea di Cione known as Orcagna (1359) to whom the splendid rose window in the facade is attributed (doubts have been expressed because the artist's sojourn in Orvieto lasted only up to 1361, and he seems to have worked mainly on the mosaic decoration.). However, observation of the elegant execution of this immense piece of lacework in marble, seems to indicate that Orcagna not only provided the design but also worked on it himself, leaving the rest of the work, which continued for years, to the ordinary stone cutters. Unfortunately lightning also struck this great rose window in 1795 and the stained glass was totally

▼ The rose window in the facade, attributed to Orcagna

destroyed. Valadier, who was rebuilding the right spire, was also called in to renew the marble decoration and he most probably designed the new stained glass as well.

Between 1451 and 1456 another Sienese, Antonio Federighi, successor of *capomastro* Giovannino di Meuccio contadino, left his mark on the facade. Although he grafted Renaissance modules such as the twelve small aedicules over the rose window onto the facade, he did not actually alter the allover Gothic style. For some reason he left his post in 1456 and the documents tell us that Giovannino di Meuccio once more took over in 1460. Lastly Michele Sanmicheli, well into the sixteenth century, continued the work, on the whole maintaining the original style, with the middle cusp and then those at the sides (1513/1532). Despite the passing of time, then, the facade of the cathedral of Orvieto is basically uniform in style, as if it had been built in just a few years, enriched with its varicolored marbles, sculpture in marble and bronze, and the colorful mosaics. *Capomastro* in 1381 of the mosaic work was Piero di Puccio from Orvieto. Unfortunately the original fourteenth-century mosaics (some of which were even sent to Rome as hom-

▼ Mosaic with the Coronation of the Virgin (1713) in the central gable of the facade

▲ Mosaic with the Baptism of Christ in the gable of the left portal

age to Pope Pius VI, while others found their way abroad), were drastically restored, not to say completely redone, in the eighteenth and nineteenth centuries by Roman mosaic workers. The scene with the *Coronation of the Virgin Mary* (1713/1714), for instance, in the central gable was copied in fresco and in a panel painting by Sano di Pietro, the former now in the Palazzo Pubblico in Siena, the latter in the National Picture Gallery there. The scene in the left-hand gable depicts the *Marriage of the Virgin*, with the *Presentation of Mary in the Temple* in the right-hand gable. The one over the left portal depicts the *Baptism of Christ,* with the *Assumption of Mary in Glory* in the center, and the *Nativity of Mary* over the right-hand portal. This was one of the best preserved and went to the Vatican and was then sold by dealers to the Victoria and Albert Museum in London, where it is now. If there is anything in the facade which seems a bit disturbing, it might be these mosaics in an academic-eighteenth/nineteenth-century purist style.

The bronzes, on the other hand, attributed to Maitani and his numerous collaborators and followers, and dating to between 1325 and 1330, are

still in place. The original gilding is obviously no longer there. Above the piers are the *Symbols of the Four Evangelists*, the *Angel*, the *Ox*, the *Lion* and the *Eagle*. The sculptural group, originally over the central portal, with large bronze *angels* pulling aside the curtains of a pavilion to reveal the marble figure of the *Virgin and Child* has been removed for restoration. It will eventually be on exhibit in the Museo dell'Opera, while a copy will be set over the portal. The *Virgin*, a marvelous work, has been attributed to Andrea Pisano, although various illustrious art historians believe the style is not in harmony with the work of this artist who may simply have helped renew the color. They feel it might be more appropriate to indicate Vitale Maitani, Lorenzo's son, as the artist, dating it to around 1325. The bronze *Agnus Dei* or Lamb of God high up on the central gable above the portal was made in 1352 by Matteo di Ugolino da Bologna. The gilded bronze statue of *Saint Michael* (1356) on top of the gable of the left door is also attributed to him. The statue on the right gable is by an unknown artist.

The marble statues set in small aedicules around the central rose window were made by fourteenth and fifteenth-century artists (the twelve *Prophets* on either side of the rose window) and sixteenth-century artists (above the rose window) such as Vico and Ippolito Scalza, Moschino son of Simone Mosca, Raffaello di Baccio da Montelupo, Fabiano Toti and others. They were frequently restored and at least two (Saint John and Saint James) were in large part redone at the end of the eighteenth century by the

▲ The symbols of the Evangelists, fourteenth-century bronze figures on the four piers of the facade, attributed to Lorenzo Maitani and his workshop

Roman marble worker Vincenzo Pacetti.

No question about it though that the marble reliefs depicting stories of the Old and New Testament on the four piers on either side of the three portals are among the most famous of all of fourteenth-century sculpture. They have always been attributed to Lorenzo Maitani and collaborators such as Nicola Nuti, Meo Nuti, Vitale Maitani and with more specific reminiscences of northern sculpture, the little known Sienese Ramo di Paganello who however arrived from "beyond the Alps". Ramo was also an architect and sculptor of the cathedral and some art historians believe he was the architect and that Fra Bevignate was only the administrator of the great Orvieto cathedral construction yard. However Maitani (the so-called "Maestro Sottile" for some scholars) must himself have worked on the panels on the facade, especially those on the first pier on the left. The delicate transparency of the relief, a vague pictorial quality obtained by the subtle chiaroscuro contrasts, the "delicate" or "subtle" (*sottile*) modeling of the forms which seem to have been molded from ductile clay, create an effect of fragility never before achieved in sculpture except perhaps by another Sienese fourteenth-century artist, Giovanni d'Agostino, who offers equally spell-bound visions in his marble sculp-

▲ Bas-reliefs with stories of the Old Testament on the first pier of the facade, attributed to Lorenzo Maitani and his workshop

tures. It leads one to think that both Maitani and Giovanni d'Agostino carefully studied the musical quality of the painting of their great fellow citizen, Simone Martini, who left at least three polyptychs in Orvieto. Two of them, unfortunately no longer complete, are now in the Museo dell'-Opera del Duomo, while the third, sold in the mid 1800s, was expatriated from the church of San Francesco and is now one of the fine pieces in the Gardner Museum in Boston.

left with stories of the Old Testament. From bottom moving upwards: Creation of the world and of man – God infuses life into Adam and takes a rib from him as he sleeps; Creation of Eve; Eden with God the Father forbidding our first ancestors to pick the fruit from the tree of good and evil; Original sin; Expulsion from Paradise; Adam tilling the earth and Eve spinning; Cain and Abel making offerings to God; Cain kills Abel; The Arts of the Trivium and the Quadrivium, Grammar and Geometry with Naomi who teaches reading, Jubal father of music and Tubal Cain with the compass.

On account of the outstanding importance of these bas-reliefs in fourteenth-century European art history, a brief description herewith follows, beginning with the first pier on the

▼ Detail of the first pier with the Creation of the Animals

▲▼ Detail of the first pier with the Creation of Adam and the Creation of Eve

Second pier: Scenes of the Old Testament referring in particular to the messianic prophesies[2]. At the center, the tree of Jesse (with the genealogy of Jesus Christ) divides the scenes, with Jesse sleeping at the base. In the small central ovals,

(2) The stories on the second pier have been interpreted in various ways. I have therefore given those supplied by the famous scholar Enzo Carli (book on the Cathedral of Orvieto, 1965), while the more recent interpretations, given in parentheses, are those taken from Eraldo Rosatelli's book ("Il duomo di Orvieto...", 2000).

▼ Detail of the second pier with Stories of the Old Testament

▲ ▼ Detail of the third pier with the Annunciation and the Adoration of the Magi

six prophets, beginning with David with the Psalter, above the Virgin Mary, Blessing Christ and John the Baptist. Beginning once more at the bottom: Adam's sepulchral urn; David anointed King by Samuel; Gideon's fleece; Balaam's prophecy (or Balaam consulting God before the destruction of Jerusalem); Balaam's ass; Israel in Egypt (or Moses' canticle of thanksgiving for the liberation of the Jews from Egypt); The Word melting the ice (or Moses saved is presented to the Pharaoh's daughter); The waters of Redemption (or God commanding Abraham to leave the city of Ur); Nabuchadnezzar's dream (or Melchizedech's offering to Abraham); Ezekiel's vision (or Roboam and Ezekiel contemplate the symbols of the Gospels); Isaiah's prophecy (or Isaiah announcing the messianic kingdom); The Foundation stone (or King Abijah against Jeroboam's rebellion); Zechariah's vision (or Punishment of Heliodoros); Micah's prophecy (or Judith on her way to the camp of Holofernes); Truth and Justice (or Baldassar's Banquet); Moses on Sinai (or Annunciation to Zechariah of the birth of John the Baptist); Prophecy of the Crucifixion; Angel greeting Mary as the prefiguration of the Annunciation.

Third pier: Scenes of the New Testament with, below, Abraham sleeping, numerous biblical personages. Beginning from the third register: Annunciation to Mary; Visitation; Birth of Jesus; Epiphany; Presentation in the Temple; Flight to Egypt; Massacre of the Innocents; Dispute in the Temple; Baptism of Christ; Temptation of Christ; Entry into Jerusalem; Kiss of Judas; Flagellation; Crucifixion; The Three Maries at the Tomb; Noli me tangere.

Fourth pier: Last Judgment; above, Christ the Judge, the Virgin Mary, John the Baptist, the Apostles and Prophets. The Elect, the Damned, the Resurrection of the Dead, Hell.

Installation of the sculptures on the four piers began in 1331. They must therefore have been made in the preceding years, when Maitani, who died in 1330, was working on the Cathedral and was planning the facade. As early as 1363 protective panels were added to keep the reliefs from being damaged by boys playing in the square. After the most recent vandalistic offense, shatterproof glass was set over the lower part of each panel. The three bronze doors on the facade are the latest addition, the work of Emilio Greco, one of the best known Italian sculptors of the 1900s. Orvieto has a museum that bears his name and contains many masterpieces by this artist from Catania. The scenes on the central door depict the *Works of Mercy* (1965/70). Around the corner to the left of the facade is a fine marble statue by Antonio Federighi (1456) of the *Eritrean Sybil*, while on the right

▲ Bas-relief on the fourth pier with the Last Judgment

▲▼ Detail of the fourth pier with the Resurrection of the Flesh and the Damned

▼► The central portal with the bronze doors by Emilio Greco.
Above, right, the group of bronze angels by Maitani on either side of the marble Madonna and Child, formerly attributed to Andrea Pisano and, more recently, perhaps to Vitale, Lorenzo Maitani's son.
The group is currently in the Museo dell'Opera del Duomo

▲▼ Emilio Greco, two details of the portal with the Works of Mercy

is another fine statue by Fabiano Toti (1588) of the *Libyan Sybil.*

On the right side, faced in alternating strips of white travertine and black basalt, is the so-called *Porta Postierla,* with a bronze architrave with figures of *Christ and the Apostles* in low relief, signed by a master Rosso (RUBEUS FECIT HOC OPUS), sometimes indicated as the Maestro

Rosso padellaio from Perugia, metal caster who, in 1263, placed the large gilded bronze sphere on the top of the dome of the cathedral of Siena. An interpretation of this sort however does not stand up to the facts for the architrave in Orvieto is in a fourteenth-century Florentine Gothic style, while Rosso padellaio, certainly active in 1263, was a master, and perhaps only a caster, of at least fifty years earlier.

The same interpretation applies to the lovely Porta Postierla itself, by some hypothetically thought to be the only remaining element of the original cathedral of Santa Maria, torn down in 1290 to make way for the new building. The present door with its fine marble decoration and pointed arch however indicates a fourteenth-century Gothic style.

Two doors were opened in the left flank of the cathedral, with its black/white stripes, the *Porta di Canonica,* with a fresco of the *Madonna and Child,* by Andrea di Giovanni da Orvieto (1412), in the lunette, and the *Porta del Corporale* through

◀ Antonio Federighi (15th cent.), the Eritrean Sybil

▲ Maestro Rubeus, architrave of the Porta Postierla,
on the right flank of the cathedral (14th cent.)

which, according to tradition, the blood-stained linen was first taken into the new cathedral. It is decorated with a bronze architrave showing the miracle of Bolsena, a recent work (1889) cast by Alessandro Nelli on a model by Adolfo Cozza, in a fourteenth-century Gothic style.

▶ Bronze architrave
of the Porta
del Corporale,
on the left flank
of the cathedral (1889)

INTERIOR

T he light that floods the nave and two aisles comes from windows in a clerestory and others in the aisles filled half with alabaster slabs and half with neo-Gothic stained glass (1886-1891) designed by Cav. Francesco Mo-retti. The great stained-glass quadrifore in the apse by master Giovanni di Bonino da Assisi dates to between 1328 and 1334. The original trussed timber roof of the cathedral was renewed at the end of the nineteenth century, together with the other unfortunate restorations carried out with excessive

◀▲ The interior of the Cathedral and,
in the etching,
as it was in the 19th century
before the "restoration"
carried out late in that century

zeal by the architect Paolo
Zampi. The cross vaulting in
the transept and apse however
remained. The cylindrical
columns were built of alternate
rows of basalt and travertine,
like the outside. The bottom
portion of the walls to a height
of somewhat more than three
feet was also decorated in this
way, and the rest remained
bare, perhaps in preparation
for frescoes which were never
done. In the late eighteenth
century, after various sixteenth-
century paintings had been destroyed in the "restoration"

process, the black and white stripes were painted up to the top of the walls.

At the beginning of the nave is a fine marble *holy water stoup* by Antonio Federighi from

◀▼ Giovanni di Bonino, details of the stained-glass window (14th cent.) in the apse

Siena. As mentioned he was also *capomastro* of the cathedral construction yard in Orvieto between 1451 and 1456. In the right aisle, is another modern *holy water stoup* by Camillo Cardinali. The five chapels in the aisle wall were originally decorated with frescoes, replaced in the late sixteenth century by stucco altars, which were in turn destroyed by the nineteenth-century "restoration" which ostensibly was attempting to return the church to its original pristine condition. The fourteenth and fifteenth-century frescoes, including some by Pietro di Puccio, known as "Grana" da Orvieto (known for his frescoes in the Camposanto in Pisa), came back to light in a fragmentary condition, but enough to tell us they were fairly mediocre. The large paintings which had been made for the altars were removed and are now in the museum of the Opera del Duomo. The only pictures remaining after this defacement were documented by the photographer Luigi Armoni in 1877.

A *wrought iron gate* (1337) signed by Conte di Lello Orlandi, a well-known iron worker from Siena, closes off the right arm of the transept. At the back, on the right, beyond a second *gate* signed by Maestro Gismondo da Orvieto and dated 1516, is the entrance to the fa-

▶ Antonio Federighi, holy water stoup (15th cent.)

mous Cappella Nuova (1408/1444), better known as SAN BRIZIO CHAPEL, entirely lined with frescoes by Fra Angelico, Gozzoli and Luca Signorelli from Cortona. Fra Angelico began work, together with Benozzo Gozzoli, in 1447, but he painted only the two vault sections with *Christ in Judgment, Angels and Prophets.* Work soon came to a halt and not until 1489 was Perugino

▼ The San Brizio Chapel with frescoes by Fra Angelico, Benozzo Gozzoli and Signorelli

▲ San Brizio Chapel, Fra Angelico, Christ the Judge

approached. He never began and finally, on April 5, 1499, Luca Signorelli was called in to continue Fra Angelico's decoration. By 1504 the artist from Cortona with his school had finished painting the entire chapel.

Luca Signorelli's frescoes in Orvieto are the masterpiece of this famous Italian Renaissance artist (although his frescoes in the cloister of the Abbey of Monteoliveto Maggiore, near Siena, should not be forgotten). Never before in painting had there been such an expressive force in the frantic tangle of imposing bodies, in the infernal monsters or the monumentality of the figures of the Elect. These three-dimensional volumes, grafted one onto the other, or isolated in space, form an organic pictorial architecture that fills the observer with amazement and at the same time a dramatic unease as if he himself were participating in this immense human tragedy. For the sake of brevity we will do no more than mention the decoration in the vault sections, with the *Apostles*, the *Angels bearing the instruments of the Passion (premonitory signs of the Last Judgment)*, *Martyrs, Patriarchs, Doctors of the Church* and the *Choir of Virgins*. In reading the paintings on the walls, the best place to begin is the large lunette to the left upon entering, with the *Preaching of the Antichrist*. In this splendid landscape the Antichrist also appears in the background, cast down to earth with his acolytes in a rain of fire sent down by the archangel Michael. In the corner on the left of the scene are the figures of Fra Angelico and Signorelli shown as they were in their noble vestment. The Antichrist, with the devil whispering in his ear, is surrounded by a host

of figures. One of them is obviously Dante, but identification of the others varies. It has been suggested that the bald older man standing on the Antichrist's right is Christopher Columbus, and others include Boccaccio, Petrarch, the young

◄▲ San Brizio Chapel, Luca Signorelli, *Preaching of the Antichrist* and a detail with the portraits of Signorelli and Fra Angelico

Raphael with a red cap, Cesare Borgia, Giovan Paolo Baglioni, a Monaldeschi from Orvieto ... but it is best to use your imagination.

The second scene in line with the events is the one over the entrance which shows the *End of the World* as cities collapse

▲ San Brizio Chapel, Luca Signorelli, the End of the World

in ruins and terrified people flee under a darkening sky with stars falling from the heavens. Below are the Sybil and the prophets of the end of the world. To be noted in this breath-taking work are the exceptional perspective effects of the bodies on the ground, and the monumental fleeing figures, three-dimensional forms moving through space.

The third scene, opposite the Antichrist, is of the *Resurrection of the Flesh* with skeletons and bodies struggling to free themselves from the earth. The movements of each figure can be followed as ever so slowly they emerge from the ground and take on flesh, powerful immobile plastic forms.

In the fourth scene *The Damned are taken to Hell and Received by the Demons*. A frightening tangle of bodies of Dantesque memory, a tremendous

▼ San Brizio Chapel, Luca Signorelli, the Resurrection of the Flesh

twisting and contortion in which the bodies become one in a single great composition. In the center, the coveted prey with the *Whore of the Apocalypse* taken to hell by a flying demon.

The fifth and sixth scenes on the back wall, on either side of the altar, show the *Reprobates driven to Hell*, on the right, a splendid and terrible pictorial translation of Dante's Gates of Hell with the shore of the river Acheron, Charon ferrying the damned across and

◀▲ San Brizio Chapel, Luca Signorelli, the Damned sent to Hell and a detail with the Whore of the Apocalypse

Minos judging them. On the left: the *Elect being led to Paradise by angels.*

The seventh scene on the left wall, next to that of the Antichrist, shows the *Elect on their way to Paradise.* The luminous atmosphere is filled with the musical movement of the angels, the statuesque positions of the nudes who, here, in Orvieto once more take their place in the History of Art, only slightly more formal when compared with Michelangelo's dramatic nudes in the Sistine chapel and his marble sculptures for the tomb of Pope Julius.

Observing the frescoes we cannot help but think of the

multitude of drawings no longer extant (except for a few particularly fine ones in the Uffizi in Florence) which Signorelli must have made, probably from life, for the preparation of the frescoes. Each figure is shown in a different position, from the front, the back, in profile, and the artist must have used real living models.

In the lower part of the chapel

▲▼ San Brizio Chapel,
Luca Signorelli,
detail with the Reprobates and the Elect

walls, just as carefully composed, Luca Signorelli depicted the philosophers and poets of antiquity in many smaller panels. *Empedocles, Homer, Lucano, Horace, Virgil, Ovid* and once more *Dante* can be identified. Next to them many of the small scenes with historical and mythological subjects are taken with great imagination from the *Divine Comedy*. They bear witness to the enduring interest in Dante's text and confirm the secular and classical aspects of Renaissance Humanism, in addition to the ever present religious feelings. The

▼ San Brizio Chapel, Luca Signorelli, the Elect in Paradise

▲ San Brizio Chapel, Luca Signorelli, Dante

eto) that this imposing cathedral was built to preserve the linen on which drops of blood had fallen when the host was consecrated in the small church in Bolsena. In the niche Signorelli painted a *Pietà* and the two saints, perhaps his last work, dating to around 1504 after finishing the great pictorial undertaking of the chapel, a fundamental text for Italian Renaissance art and the prelude to what a few years later was to be an even greater undertaking, Michelangelo's Sistine Chapel.

At the center of the Baroque altar in the Chapel of San Brizio (Bernardino Cametti, 1715) is the so-called Madonna di San Brizio. This panel painting of the Madonna Enthroned with the Child, Angels, and the head of Christ in the gable is probably by a late thirteenth-century master from Orvieto to whom art historians have attributed numerous works, particularly frescoes (the quality of those in the church of San Giovenale is noteworthy), a master who was influenced by the Florentine painting of Cimabue and Coppo di Marcovaldo. Unfortunately the panel suffered damage in the past and the face of the Child is a repainting of the fourteenth century. The Madonna of San Brizio is so-called because leg-

stories, also set into architectural panels, refer to Virgil's *Aeneid*, the more or less mythological episodes of *Orpheus and Euridice, Hercules, Persephone and Pluto, Perseus and Andromeda*, etc. If the visitor has enough time, he can identify many. We must however also mention the small wall *chapel of the Corpi Santi* or Saints Faustino and Pietro Parenzo to the right of the entrance where the mortal remains of these saints were contained in a casket. Pietro Parenzo, podestà of Orvieto in 1199, was killed by the Patarines, a community which denied the sacrament of the Eucharist. Perhaps it was to contradict this doctrine declared heretical by the Church (but popular in Orvi-

end says that this saint left it to the Orvietani he evangelized as a gift. Which also explains why the Cappella Nuova is more commonly known as the Chapel of San Brizio. Recent exploration carried out during restoration also verified the fact that portions of Signorelli's frescoes were destroyed when the eighteenth-century altar was built.

Right outside the Chapel of San Brizio, on the right, is the *Chapel of the Magi* (1538-46) with the large relief of the *Adoration of the Magi* by Raffaello di Baccio da Montelupo on the marble altar.

Equally fine is the decoration of the sanctuary and the apse. A large polychrome wooden *Crucifix* attributed to Maitani and collaborator hangs over the high altar. This Sienese artist left three large polychrome wooden crucifixes in Orvieto: this one, one in the sacristy of the cathedral, and the third in the church of San Francesco.

The wooden *choir stalls* along the walls of the apse, restored and in part redone in 1859 (some of the inlays, including the large panel with the Coronation of the Virgin, were at the time moved to the Museo dell'Opera), still reveal their Gothic origins. They were begun in 1329 by Giovanni Ammannati (or Ammannato) and a group of Sienese wood

▼ Chapel of the Magi, Raffaello di Baccio da Montelupo, Adoration of the Magi

▲ Ugolino di Prete Ilario, detail of the apse frescoes with the Prophets and Saint John the Baptist

carvers including Nicola Nuti, Ambrogino di Meo, Jacopo di Lotto. Up to around 1540 they were in the center of the nave. When they were transferred to the apse, the painted decorations on the exterior were lost.

Another great undertaking of late Gothic style was the fresco series with the *Stories of the Life of the Virgin* in the apse. The stories are based on the apocryphal Gospels and work was begun in 1370 by Ugolino di Prete Ilario from Orvieto and numerous collaborators including Cola Petruccioli and Andrea di Giovanni. Note the great difference between this cycle by Ugolino and the one, just discussed, by Luca Sig-norelli. The latter, even in the calmer and more monumental scenes, forcefully and dramatically cries out the final destiny of humanity, while the former, still medieval in feeling, narrates a charming tale where men and things carry out their assigned roles in peace and quiet. In these serene visions the influence of contemporary Sienese painting is evident in the way in which Giotto's great lesson is modified into rhythmical lines and rich colors. At the end of the fifteenth century Antonio di Massaro from Perugia, known as Pastura, redid the two scenes below on the right with the *Annunciation* and the *Visitation*.

In the left arm of the transept, companion to the Chapel of the Magi, is the *Chapel of the Visitation* with the marble altar by Simone Mosca and Raffaello di Baccio da Montelupo, with a marble high relief of the *Visitation* by Francesco Mosca, known as Moschino (or little Mosca) since he was son of Simone. Next to the pier of the crossing is the imposing marble group of the *Pietà*, signed by Ippolito Scalza and dated 1579. This spectacular work seems to have been inspired by

▼ Ugolino di Prete Ilario, detail of the apse frescoes with the Presentation of Mary in the Temple and Joseph leading Mary to his House

Michelangelo, although it is overly theatrical and therefore not as emotionally powerful.

At the back of the left transept is the famous **CHAPEL OF THE BLESSED CORPORAL**, set into the flying buttress erected by Maitani, and right across from the Chapel of St. Brizio.

The two sixteenth-century statues of the *Resurrected Christ* and the *Virgin Mary* on either side of the entrance are by Raffaello di Baccio da Montelupo.

The fourteenth-century Chapel of the Corporal (1350/1356) is closed by a *wrought iron gate* by Matteo di Ugolino da Bologna, between 1355 and 1362, and finished in 1364 by Giovanni di Micheluccio da Orvieto. The chapel was built specifically to house the blood-stained linen or corporal from Bolsena, still there on a fine altar which may in part be the work of Orcagna.

But what captures the visitor's attention is the RELIQUARY originally made for the corporal and the fragments of host, now turned to dust. One remains speechless in front of this

◄ Ippolito Scalza, the great "Pietà" (1579)

splendid reliquary in silver, gilded silver and translucent glowing enamel which seems to have been inspired by the facade of the cathedral. It dates to between 1337 and 1338 and is without question the absolute masterpiece of the famous Sienese goldsmith Ugolino di Vieri as well as one of the outstanding extant examples of European Gothic goldwork.

A few details regarding this truly

▼ Ugolino di Vieri,
Reliquary of the Corporal (1337-1338)

exceptional piece are given here. It is over a meter high, in the form of a triptych. Silver, and gilded silver, plaques are set into the solid silver reliquary, with 24 scenes of the life of Christ and 8 stories regarding the corporal. All the scenes reveal the influence of late thirteenth and early fourteenth-century French goldwork. Current art historians also tend to see influences of this sort in late thir-

▼ Ugolino di Vieri, detail of the enamels on the reliquary of the Corporal with the bishop receiving the blood-stained altar cloth

teenth and early-fourteenth century Sienese painting and sculpture as well. The plaques are covered by vari-colored translucent enamel, a Sienese specialty up to well into the fifteenth century, to lend greater splendor and luminosity to this marvelous work. It cost 1374 and a half gold florins and was carried in procession for the first time for the feast of Corpus Christi in 1338. On the base is a long in-

▼ Ugolino di Vieri, detail of the enamels on the reliquary of the Corporal with the Entry of Christ into Jerusalem

scription with the name of the patrons and the artist:

+ HOC OPUS FECIT FIERI DOMINUS FRATER TRAMUS EPISCOPUS URBETANUS ET D[ominus] ANGELUS ARCHIPRESBITERI ET D[ominus] LIGUS CAPELANUS DOMINI PAPE ET D[ominus] NICHOLAUS D[e] ALATRO ET D[ominus] FREDUS ET D[ominus] NINUS ET D[ominus] LEONARDUS CANONECI URBETANI + PER MAGISTRUM UGOLINUM ET SOTIOS AURIFICIES DE SENIS FACTUM FUIT SUB ANNO DOMINI MCCCXXXVIII TEMPORE DOMINI BENEDICTI PAPE XII +

As noted in the inscription, Ugolino also had his "*sotios*", collaborators whom art historians today indicate as the Sienese Tondino di Guerrino and Andrea Riguardi. The scenes on the plaques reflect the Sienese Gothic and lose nothing in comparison with the great painting of the time in the city, in particular by Pietro and Ambrogio Lorenzetti, to which they are close in style.

There is also a panel painting of considerable historical and artistic interest in the Chapel of the Corporal. This is a venerated image known as the *Madonna dei Raccomandati*, painted around 1320 by another famous Sienese painter, Lippo Memmi, a close collaborator of Simone Martini whose daughter he married. The splendid panel is signed "Lipus de Sena nat. Nos picxit amena". The frescoes on the wall are once more by Ugolino di Prete Ilario and collaborators, including Pietro di Puccio known as "Grana". They were painted earlier (1357/64) than the cycle in the apse but since they had deteriorated, they were repainted around the middle of the nineteenth century. Restoration has revealed the original portions. The scenes show *Stories of the Bible*, the *Eucharist*, *Christ* with a *Crucifixion* signed by Ugolino in 1364, the *Miracle of Bolsena* and the *Consecrated Host,* etc.

The imposing setting for the *organ* above the chapel was designed by Ippolito Scalza around 1582/84. The *gate* that closes the left aisle is another fine work by Conte di Lello Orlandi, signed and dated 1338, a year later, then, than the gate on the right aisle.

The chapels in this aisle wall were also once covered with fourteenth-century frescoes, destroyed when the stucco altars were set there, which in turn were destroyed at the end of the nineteenth century. The frescoes that reappeared were fragmentary and worn. Fortunately a masterpiece near the entrance was saved, perhaps because it was by a famous artist. This is the delicate fresco with the *Madonna Enthroned*

▲ Lippo Memmi, the Madonna dei Raccomandati (of Mercy) (1320)

and Child, painted by Gentile da Fabriano in 1425, one of the best-known and most illustrious late Gothic Italian painters, mentioned in all art history books for his great panel with the Adoration of the Magi, in the Uffizi Gallery in Florence. Recent restoration has revealed an almost transparent *angel*

▼ Gentile da Fabriano, Madonna and Child (1425)

that is pure spirit on the Virgin's left.

Mention must also be made of the large marble *baptismal font* set under the first arch of the aisle and supported by crouching lions, begun by still another Sienese artist, Luca di Giovanni, around 1390 and with a red marble basin made (per-

haps for the second time) by a certain Pietro di Giovanni from Freiburg and continued by other sculptors, last of whom was Sano di Matteo with the octagonal pyramid, signed by him and dated 1407.

► Luca di Giovanni, Pietro di Giovanni from Freiburg and Sano di Matteo, the baptismal font (1390-1407)

THE MUSEUMS AROUND PIAZZA DEL DUOMO

Once more back in Piazza del Duomo we have *Palazzo Faina* across from the cathedral. Housed here are the **Museo Civico Archeologico** and the **Museo Claudio Faina**, also an archaeological museum dedicated to Claudio Faina who donated the rich family collection of thousands of objects pertaining to Etruscan and Greek culture to the City of Orvieto in 1954. The two sections hold important artifacts, many of which from the Etruscan necropoli in the territory of Orvieto, the Belvedere Temple, the sacred area of Cannicella, etc. To note particularly on the ground floor is the *sarcophagus* with scenes in bas-relief with traces of color from Torre San Severo. This exceptional piece dates to the fourth century B.C. with scenes depicting sacrifices of ancient Greek mythology: Sacrifice of Polyxena, Achilles sacrificing Trojan prisoners in honor of his friend Patrocles, Ulysses sacrificing a ram, Ulysses with Circe and his companions transformed into beasts. Of particular note are a funerary cippus in the form of the head of a warrior (6th century B.C.), antefixes and terracotta sculpture from the Temple of Belvedere, the so-called Venus of Cannicella, a small figure found in this sanctuary and dating to around 530 B.C. The marble used indicates that the figure came from Greece although it is unusual to find a nude female figure in the archaic Greek period.

◄ Museo Civico Archeologico, Palazzo Claudio Faina, acroterion with the head of a Gorgon (5th cent. B.C.) from the Temple of Belvedere

▼ Museo Civico Archeologico, Palazzo Claudio Faina, the "Venus of Cannicella" (c 530 B.C.)

▶ Museo Civico Archeologico, Palazzo Claudio Faina, head of a warrior (6th cent. B.C.)

There are countless vases in the museum, often of exceptional importance and rarity, examples of ancient Greek vase painting, Corinthian and Attic (6th, 5th cent. B.C.), as fine as any to be found in the greatest archaeological museums in the world.

These vases (craters, chalices, oinochoai, lekythoi, amphorae, kantharoi, etc) with black-figure or red-figure decorations are important for they were painted, and sometimes signed, by the best Greek potters: Douris, Exekias, the Amasis painter, the Andokides painter, Lisippides, Nikostenes, etc. These Corinthian and Attic Greek ceramics, aside from their elegance, furnish us with an idea

◄ Museo Archeologico Claudio Faina, Attic black-figure amphora, by the painter Exekias (4th cent. B.C.)

of what the great Greek wall painting, which has been almost totally destroyed together with the buildings, was like. Collections of Etruscan goldwork, coins, etc. are flanked in the Faina Museum by locally produced pottery, such as the magnificent red-figure amphorae of the 4th century B.C. of the so-called "Vanth Group", named after the Etruscan winged female figures with serpents who were part of the Etruscan underworld.

The *State Archives* with a wealth of ancient documents, bullas, codices, etc. are to the right of the Palazzo Faina.

▼ Museo Archeologico Claudio Faina, Etruscan amphora of the "Vanth group" (4th cent. B.C.)

▲ First Papal Palace, currently seat of the Museo Archeologico Nazionale

Orvieto also has another archaeological museum, the **Museo Archeologico Nazionale**, temporarily housed in the first *Papal Palace* at the back of the square next to or more properly set against the right transept of the cathedral. The three great pointed arches on the ground floor and the three trifores above are the result of the most recent attempt to restore this imposing thirteenth-cen-

► The left side of the first Papal Palace, with the original trifores

▲ Museo Nazionale Archeologico on the ground floor of the first Papal Palace

tury building to its original medieval forms.

The archaeological sector contains many finds, mostly Etruscan, but also some examples of Greek art: of note the *architectural terracottas* from the Temple of Belvedere.

Of great interest is the reconstruction of the *Golini Tombs* with the original paintings that bear comparison to the much more famous ones from the Etruscan necropolis of Tarquinia. These tombs were discovered at the Necropolis of Sette Camini. The Museo Archeologico Nazionale will probably be moved definitively to Palazzo

◄ Museo Nazionale Archeologico, polychrome terra cotta antefix from the Temple of Belvedere

▲▶ Museo Archeologico Nazionale, wall paintings from the so-called Golini Tombs

Crispo, now headquarters of the financial offices. Some of the works of the important MUSEO DELL'OPERA DEL DUOMO will be installed in the other Papal Palace, better known as *Palazzo Soliano*. This is also a massive building, almost a fortress, with the facade on the square and its side parallel to that of the cathedral. It was commissioned at the end of the thirteenth century by Boniface VIII of Dantesque fame, as an addition to the first papal palace, with an imposing hall on the upper floor, access to which is by an external

▲ The Papal Palace known as Palazzo Soliano, seat of the Museo dell'Opera del Duomo

staircase at the side. Light comes in through three-light windows. Work was not finished until the fifteenth century when it was covered, but once more the architect Paolo Zampi, with that typical nineteenth-century mania to redo, altered the original structure with an ugly addition in brick and false Guelph battlements which are still there.

The Museo dell'Opera will be installed in the two papal palaces. The countless works of art, paintings, sculpture, goldwork, etc., in the museum

◄ Trifore of Palazzo Soliano

will include outstanding masterpieces. Presumably the museum will be opened in installments, as the exhibition rooms are restructured. Since no definitive itinerary can be indicated, we will choose a few of the most important works, beginning with the two precious fourteenth-century *drawings*, on parchment, with the facade of the cathedral, one of which is attributed to Maitani.

Outstanding paintings include the panel with the *Madonna Enthroned and Child,* a rare work by the Spoleto artists Simeone and Machilone, dating to around the middle of the thirteenth century and considered one of the most important and finest examples of Umbrian painting of that century. Immediately thereafter in importance is the large *"Maestà"* or *Madonna Enthroned and Child* with two small *angels*, for-

merly in the Church of the Servi in Orvieto. Restoration brought out all the precious touches of gold and brilliant color. This is one of the most important panel paintings of the entire thirteenth century. It has traditionally been attributed to Coppo di Marcovaldo, Florentine and known follower of Cimabue, an attribution confirmed by various illustrious art historians of today, particularly in view of an almost identical copy in the Church of the

► Museo dell'Opera del Duomo, Simeone and Machilone, Madonna Enthroned and Child (13th cent.)

◀ Museo dell'Opera del Duomo, Sienese painter of the second half of the 13th century (formerly attributed to Coppo di Marcovaldo), Madonna and Child

in the city between 1260 and 1280. What we have here then is probably a magnificent work by an unknown Sienese artist, around 1270/75, influenced by Guido and by Cimabue and who had carefully observed Coppo's painting in the Servite church in Siena. To Servi in Siena. More recently though, beginning with Boskovits[3], this attribution has been challenged and with reason. To be noted is how the style tends towards the more delicate and flowing forms of Sienese painting of the second half of the thirteenth century, which centered around the art of Guido da Siena who worked

(3) M. Boskovits in "Scritti in onore di Ugo Procacci", Milan, 1977, p 95.

be noted, however, is that recent restoration has shown that the faces of the Child and of the Madonna were later retouched in oil, faithfully following the original painting underneath. In view of the high quality of this overpainting, it has not been removed.

For the fourteenth century mention must be made of the magnificent paintings by the great Sienese Simone Martini. They originally formed two polyptychs. The first is missing two of its seven panels. At the center is the *Virgin and Child* with *Saints Peter, Mary Magdalene, Paul* and *Dominic* at the sides. The small figure of the patron, Trasmundo Monaldeschi, bishop of Sovana, is shown kneeling next to the half figure of the Magdalene who presents him to the Virgin. Differences in size between the principal figures and the patron were normal in works of this time and reflected the relative unimportance of the latter when compared with the saints and other religious figures. Simone Martini signed and dated the polyptych but unfortunately the inscription is incomplete "....NE DE SENIS ME PINXIT...CCCXX..." the N is certainly the last letter of SIMON while the date must refer to a year between 1321 and 1324.

Only the central panel with

▼ Museo dell'Opera del Duomo, Simone Martini, polyptych with the Madonna and Saints Peter, Dominic, Magdalene, Paul

the *Madonna and Child,* with a *Blessing Christ* and two *angels* in the gable, remain of Simone's second polyptych. Various frag- ments are in American and European museums. However mention must be made of a third polyptych by Simone

▼ Museo dell'Opera del Duomo, Simone Martini, detail of the central panel with the Madonna and Child from a dismembered polyptych

which was in the church of San Francesco in Orvieto up to the nineteenth century. It was sold in its entirety and is now on display in the Isabella Stewart Gardner Museum in Boston.

The Museo dell'-Opera del Duomo in Orvieto also houses another masterpiece that has come down to us in a good state. This is the so-called *Reliquary of San Savino*, an exceptional example of medieval goldwork also signed by Ugolino di Vieri and his close collaborator Viva di Lando, also Sienese + UGHOLINUS ET VIVA D[E] SENIS FECIERU[N]T ISTUM TABERNACULU[M] +. It is over a meter high and consists of a polygonal base supported by lions, with a cupola which in turn supports the statuette of the Virgin and Child. Small columns which come out of the base support a small spire in pure Gothic style, like those on the fourteenth-century Gothic cathedrals. Inside the spire is the statuette of Saint Savino (the angel at the top is a nineteenth-century replacement). The stories on the reliquary refer to the life of the saint, told, as in those of the Corporal, on silver and gold plaques covered with varicolored translucent enamels. This work might have been a trial piece before the definitive assigning of the commission for the Reliquary of the Corporal.

Marble fourteenth-century sculpture includes the lovely statue of the *Virgin and Child* by Andrea Pisano, the *Blessing*

▲ Museo dell'Opera del Duomo, Andrea Pisano, Madonna and Child

brogino di Meo, collaborator in the choir of the cathedral. There are numerous fourteenth and fifteenth-century frescoes, removed from the churches in the territory. The sixteenth century will be represented by the paintings originally over the altars in the side chapels of the cathedral and assigned to Girolamo Muziano, the Zuccari brothers, Cesare Nebbia, Circignani, Lan-

Christ, also by him, formerly over the Porta del Corporale, rare fragments by Arnolfo di Cambio, including some that were once part of the monument to Cardinal de Braye in the Church of San Domenico, other works by Nicola and Nino Pisano and their school. Examples of wooden sculpture include the monumental *Blessing Christ* from Maitani's workshop, the two statues with the *Annunciation* attributed to Am-

franco etc. The great sixteenth-century statues of the *Apostles* which up to 1896 were located at the base of the columns inside the cathedral, marbles by Fabiano Toti, Scalza, Moschino, together with the two figures of Vincenzo Mochi's marvelous *Annunciation*, which was also in the cathedral, will also be on view. The large *cartoons* by Marcantonio Franceschini, models for his frescoes in a hall of the Palazzo Ducale in Genoa (1702), which were

▲ Museo dell'Opera del Duomo, Marcantonio Franceschini, drawing on paper for the lost frescoes of the Ducal Palace in Genoa

totally destroyed by fire in 1777, will also remain here.

The hall on the ground floor of the Palace of Boniface VIII currently houses the **Museum dedicated to Emilio Greco**, one of the best known of modern Italian sculptors, who made the three doors on the facade of the cathedral. The room also contains over 30 pieces of sculpture in bronze including his famous nude women, shown in various positions and modes,

◄ Museo dell'Opera del Duomo, Vincenzo Mochi, Angel of the Annunciation

◄▼ Museo Emilio Greco,
Emilio Greco, two female figures

in finely modulated rhythms and plasticity of form. Emilio Greco's "Venuses" are well known and appreciated by collectors and museums throughout the world and can be encountered in public parks and art museums of large cities in Europe and America. But perhaps for many Italians the name of Emilio Greco makes them think only of his famous monument to Pinocchio in the park of Collodi. The Emilio Greco Museum will eventually be transferred to the Palazzo Faina.

Culture, folklore, crafts

The two principal events which take place in Orvieto are primarily of a religious nature, with traditions that go far back in time: the *Feast of the Palombella* and the *Procession of Corpus Domini (Corpus Christi)*. The Palombella takes place in Piazza del Duomo on Pentecost (Whit Sunday) and resembles the famous Feast of the Colombina on Easter Sunday in Florence. At noon on the dot a white dove, symbolizing the Holy Spirit, is sent down along a wire from the drum of the Church of San Francesco to an architectural structure resembling the reliquary of St. Savinus within which the figures of the Virgin and the Apostles are gathered together. When the dove arrives firecrackers go off as the crowd cheers and pronostications are made as to what the coming year holds in store for the crops. It is truly a popular festival, with bells ringing, firecrackers, cheering, a combination of the sacred and profane so often the case in many Italian cities.

◄ The Feast of the Palombella

▼ ► Costumes for the feast
of Corpus Christi

The other event in which all Orvieto takes part is the Procession of Corpus Christi. For it was here in Orvieto that Pope Urban IV proclaimed the solemn church feast of Corpus Christi on August 11, 1264, after the miracle of Bolsena which demonstrated the Real Presence of the body of Christ in the Eucharist. Trumpeters blow their silver trumpets, drummers beat their drums as the holy blood-stained altar cloth is carried in procession through the city, accompanied by the clergy, the municipal authorities and hundreds of participants dressed in marvelous costumes representing the Magistrates of the Commune, the Capitano del Popolo, Nobles, Knights, the Guilds and the four districts into which Orvieto is divided: Corsica, Olmo, Santa Maria della Stella and Serancia.

Religious piety is joined to the more secular political sense as an age-old drama is played out and the quarters vie with each other in jousting games, common to so many other Italian cities.

Culture, folklore, crafts

Crafts too of course play an important part in the economy of the city, ranging from textiles (the famous Orvieto lace) to the pottery on display in the dozens of small shops in the town center. There are perfect imitations of famous Greek and Etruscan vases, as well as an incredible variety of other

▲ "Ars Vetana" lace (early 1900s), located in the Servizio Turistico Associato dell'Orvietano, City of Orvieto

▲ Vicolo dei Dolci

▲ Orvieto pottery

types, some purely decorative, others to be used daily. Fine imitations of the famous ceramics of Umbria or the Marches sit side by side with others based on medieval and Renaissance originals found in those "dump shafts" under the streets and now frequently in museums or private collections. Occasionally one can also find a piece in one of the many antique shops here and there in the streets of the center.

▲ Wooden sculptures in Via Michelangeli

▲ Musician angel in gilded wood inspired by Signorelli's frescoes

Orvieto is also distinguished by a particular form of crafts, that of work in wood, transformed by skillful hands into imaginary figures of people and animals.

▲ Wooden dolls by Michelangeli

The historical center
The palazzi and old churches

FIRST ITINERARY

As previously mentioned, Orvieto is still basically medieval in its features. The Romanesque and Gothic buildings have remained fairly intact throughout the centuries. An occasional Renaissance, Baroque or Neoclassic building has not greatly altered the general impression. And with the exception of a few remodelings in period style in the outskirts, they have made this splendid city all the more interesting, despite the havoc human ignorance or presumption has so often inflicted.

Let us move together then along the dark lanes and wider streets and it is up to you to choose whether to linger over a noble palazzo, the facade of an old church, a stone tower or a more modest and charming tawny colored tufa house. This palimpsest of styles is what

◄ Corso Cavour, the town's main street, leading into Piazza della Repubblica

◄ Typical views of the city

makes the historical center of Orvieto so fascinating. We will pause only before the most interesting buildings and the old churches so full of works of art, occasionally quite remarkable. Many of these buildings are unfortunately closed because of a lack of personnel, a problem common to so many historical centers in Italy.

From Piazza del Duomo let us move towards the right, down Via del Duomo, glancing up at the medieval clock tower, better known as *Torre di Maurizio* with the fourteenth-century bronze automaton at the top who strikes the hours on a bell. Art historians believe he was made by Matteo di

Ugolino da Bologna who came to Orvieto in 1351 to work for the Cathedral construction yard.

Shortly thereafter *Via del Duomo* crosses *Corso Cavour*, the main artery which runs through most of the center from east to west. A few steps from the crossing, on the left, is another tower known as *Torre del Moro*, either from the name of a "moro" or mulberry tree which grew nearby, or after a mannequin of a Saracen Moor used for target practice by Christian knights in tournaments. A few steps further on Via della Cos-

► ▼ Torre di Maurizio and the fourteenth-century bronze automaton

tituente leads to **Piazza del Popolo**, with the monumental **Palazzo del Capitano del Popolo**, in pure Romanesque style. In 1250 a new political-military figure was created in Orvieto, as it was in Florence, the Capitano del Popolo who flanked the Podestà and the Consuls in governing the city. In the last quarter of the thirteenth century the structure now before us was built, tearing down the surrounding houses and towers to create a large space in front, now Piazza del Popolo (1281-84). The palazzo has a large loggia on the ground floor with a spacious hall above. In 1316 the Campana del Popolo, or Bell of the People, was raised in the tower at the side. The building had a loggia on the front that was later closed. Two passageway arches were opened on the right side, known as Arco della Pesa. A broad flight of steps, completed by the early fourteenth century, was placed on the left side. The splendid windows on the upper floor let light into the large hall, at the time used for popular assemblies. The walls were covered with frescoes, of which only fragments remain, in part because around 1480 the original arches were replaced with a trussed timber roof. In the seventeenth century there was a pawn agency (Monte di Pietà) here and a theater was installed. At the end of the nineteenth century parts were redone, including the swallow-tail Ghi-

◀ Torre del Moro

▲ Palazzo del Capitano del Popolo

belline embattlements. Today the building is a center for meetings and exhibitions. Restructuration in the subsoil also recently revealed an archaeological area with Etruscan and medieval finds, portions of an aqueduct and a cistern.

The nineteenth-century *Palazzo Bracci* designed by Virgilio Vespignani overlooks Piazza del Popolo. Next to it is the Romanesque *church of San Rocco*, with a Renaissance portal. Inside are numerous frescoes including one of the *Virgin and Child* with *Saints* by Eusebio da Montefiascone.

Back on Corso Cavour, on the right at no. 87, is the fine *Palazzo dei Sette* (1571-76), with a noble courtyard, and where exhibitions are frequently held. The Corso leads directly to *Piazza della Repubblica*, once possibly the Etruscan and Roman forum, where past historians thought the cardo and decumanus may have crossed, a theory confirmed by some recent scholars. The imposing **City Hall** overlooks the square.

◄ The Church of San Rocco and, in the foreground, the Renaissance cistern

This early thirteenth-century building was renovated in the second half of the sixteenth century (1571-80) by Ippolito Scalza who designed the facade with the imposing arches so typical of the late Renaissance. They support a loggia with large windows in the same style. The old thirteenth-century structure is still visible at the back, while there are pointed arches inside, probably dating, like the tower, to the late thirteenth century. On the left the palace is grafted onto the twelve-sided *bell tower* of the church of Sant'Andrea, with narrow bifores which, in the upper zone, form three closely set tiers, much

▼ The City Hall

like those in the campanile of the Abbey of Santi Severo e Martirio outside the city. The *Church of Sant'Andrea* next to it acts as backdrop for one end of the square. In the Middle Ages this was one of the most important civil and religious sites in the city, where pacts and alliances were stipulated, bishops and cardinals were cre- ated, where the lords of the surrounding area came each year, on August 15th, to swear allegiance to the Comune. The first early Christian church was erected in the sixth century on what may have been an Etr-

▼ Church of Sant'Andrea and its twelve-sided bell tower

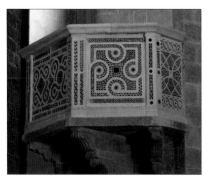

▲ Church of Sant'Andrea,
Cosmati masters, mosaics on the pulpit

uscan sacred area. The remains of this church, with a fine mosaic floor, can be seen about two meters under the present church. As we see it now, San-

▼ Church of Sant'Andrea,
interior with the Magalotti Tomb
(14th cent.) in the foreground

t'Andrea is basically twelfth century, completed in the fourteenth, and with the nave renovated in the early sixteenth century. A drastic restoration of 1926 falsified both the facade and the bell tower making them look almost brand new. The mediocre bas relief in the lunette over the portal is also recent. The interior still has the basilica plan with a nave and two aisles separated by tall columns in oriental granite (perhaps reused classic material) with sixteenth-century capitals which support the round-headed arches and the timber truss roof, while cross vaulting is set over the transept. The interesting *pulpit* is also composed of material that has been re-employed, with one slab inside and three slabs dec-

orated outside with patterns which are typical of sixth and seventh-century Ravenna. The exterior mosaic decorations recall the art of the twelfth and thirteenth-century Cosmati masters.

Followers of Arnolfo di Cambio sculpted the large *Magalotti aedicule tomb* in pure Gothic style and with a fresco of the *Madonna and Child*, reminiscent of the Lorenzetti and Sienese art. There are also various frescoes on the walls, some better preserved than others, by Orvieto artists of the fourteenth and fifteenth centuries.

Our itinerary continues along *Via Filippeschi* and *Via Malabranca,* medieval in feeling and possibly once part of the decumanus which began at Porta Maggiore, at the bottom of the nearby Via della Cava. The two streets have interesting buildings in tufa or basalt, dating to the thirteenth and fourteenth centuries. Narrow lanes

(Via dell'Olmo, Via del Paradiso, etc.) with pointed or round-arched doors and windows lead off on either side, as one charming view follows another, with an occasional supporting arch crossing overhead. This is one of the most characteristic parts of the city, with a few rare Renaissance buildings. In Via Malabranca at n. 22 is the *Palazzo Filippeschi- Petrangeli* with a fine fifteenth-century courtyard, attributed by Vasari to the great Bernardo Rossellino. At n. 15 is the large sixteenth-century *Palazzo Caravajal Simoncelli*, still another work by Ippolito Scalza, with a curious inscription running

▶ Via Malabranca

San Giovenale is one of the most important medieval religious buildings in Orvieto. The first small church must have been built in the 7th-8th century, set, according to a tradition, on a pagan temple dedicated to Jove (Giove-Giovenale, although Giovenale was a bishop of Narni). The present church dates to

▲ The Renaissance courtyard
of Palazzo Filippeschi Petrangeli

▼ The fourteenth century portal
of the former church of Sant'Agostino

along below the first row of windows "Caravaial de Caravajal por comodidad de sus amigos padron". And then *Piazza San Giovenale*. On the right is the flank of the former *church of Sant'Agostino* with a fine typically Gothic fourteenth-century portal, on the left a large pointed arch, also Gothic in style, which serves as entrance to a modern restaurant. *Via Volsinia* leads us to the facade of *San Giovenale* overlooking the valley below.

the beginning of the year thousand (1004?) in the form of a Lombard basilica. It was frequently renovated, particularly in the Baroque period, with mediocre decorations which were removed in the latest restorations which attempted to give the church its original form. Dozens of frescoes were discovered on the walls and columns, some of which are particularly fine.

In the restoration the simple facade lost the architrave of the portal which now has a round-arched lunette. The bell tower, also rebuilt and raised more than once, was set on the foundations of a squat defense tower which overlooked the valley of the Riochiaro right

▼ Church of San Giovenale

▲ Church of San Giovenale, lunette of the side portal with a bas-relief of 1497 depicting Saint Giovenale

below. A Renaissance type doorway was set into the massive right flank of the church, dated MCCCC97, with a mediocre stone bas-relief of *Saint Giovenale* in the lunette.

The interior consists of a nave separated from the two side aisles by squat powerful cylindrical columns with round-headed arches in Romanesque style. The cylindrical apse and transept were torn down in the thirteenth-fourteenth century and a new one was built with two spacious pointed arches supported by piers. Most of the old sacred furnishings which documented the wealth of this important Orvieto church in the Middle Ages have disappeared. The famous Reliquary of Saint Savinus was once here. The *altar* remains however, with the front consisting of a rare slab of sixth-seventh century Byzantine interlace, probably salvaged from the older small church. The corners of the altar consist of small marble pilasters with interesting figured capitals which have been connected, on account of their curious symbolism, to the Patarine

◄ Church of San Giovenale, small capital on the altar (12th cent.)

doctrine which was widespread in Orvieto and which denied the miracle of transubstantiation. The altar, only later recomposed, was made for an "Abate Guido" in 1170 by a "Maestro Bernardo" as is to be read on the side. The marble *lectern* is also a fine thirteenth-century piece with the eagle of St. John supporting the lectern table while the ox, angel and lion of the other three Evangelists are immediately below.

The vast cycle of frescoes in San Giovenale, discovered under layers of plaster, are in a sense a museum of thirteenth and fourteenth-century painting in Orvieto. Examples of the second half of the thirteenth century are rare, especially those attributed to the so-called Master of the Madonna of San Brizio, the Orvieto painter who

▲ Church of San Giovenale, the thirteenth century marble lectern

worked at the turn of the century. Of particular importance for their quality and rarity are the frescoes depicting a *Con-*

▼ Church of San Giovenale, Giovanni di Buccio Leonardelli (?), Annunciation and Nativity

version of Saint Paul, a few representations of the *Madonna Enthroned and Child*, including one, in slightly better condition, under an aedicule in Gothic style with the Bishop Saints Savinus and Giovenale at the sides. Close to this painter is a fresco on the wall near the main entrance, with a rare iconography of the *Tree of Life*. Just as important and of fine quality are the thirteenth-century frescoes attributed to the so-called Master of the Abbey of Santi Severo and Martirio, in particular those on the smooth walls of the first two columns in the church and depicting the *Annunciation*, the *Visitation* and *Jesus Crucified between His Mother Mary, Saint John and Saints Francis and Dominic*. We believe that these frescoes together with those in the Abbey of Santi Severo e

◄ Church of San Giovenale, Maestro dell'Abbazia (13th cent.), Crucifixion with the Mourning Virgin and Saint John

▲ Church of San Giovenale, Umbro-Sienese artist of the second half of the 14th century, Madonna del Latte (Nursing Madonna)

Martirio are among the most important examples of art in Orvieto of the second half of the thirteenth century[4].

With regards to fourteenth-century painting, in San Giovenale mention must be made of a delicate but fragmentary *Madonna del Latte*, or Nursing Madonna, of the second half of the century, various works attributed to Giovanni di Balduccio (or Buccio) Leonardelli, betraying the influence of the contemporary and better known Sienese painting, once more of the second half of the fourteenth century, and paintings attributed to Ugolino di Prete Ilario, Andrea di Giovanni, Cola Petruccioli, Pietro di Puccio. Panel paintings include a small *Madonna and Child* by a particulary conservative painter, in Byzantine style despite its fourteenth century dating. It is in poor state and therefore difficult to interpret. A larger altarpiece with the *Madonna Enthroned with Child and Saints*, signed by Pier Paolo Lensini, dates to the second half of the sixteenth century. A visit to San Giovenale is therefore of great

(4) On thirteenth-century painting in Orvieto, see the bibliography in: C. Fratini, Il maestro della Madonna di San Brizio e le vicende della pittura n Orvieto fra Duecento e primo Trecento. In "PARAGONE" 1989, n. 473.

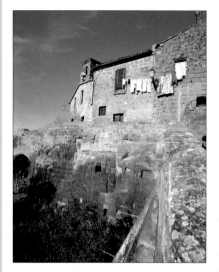

◄ Via Volsinia 2

walk along the bastions of the cliff which drop down sheer at this point and look out over a stupendous panorama. This is a must for any visitor for where else can one get such an almost aerial spectacle. Via Volsinia 2 leads to the **Porta Maggiore** below, the oldest entrance dating to Etruscan/Roman times. To reach it one must leave the bastions for the steep Via Malcorini and climb up the *Via Cava* (possibly one of the first tracts of the decumanus), certainly one of the oldest and most interesting streets in Orvieto. Continuing, on the right,

interest to both scholar and tourist.

From San Giovenale, along Via Volsinia 2, we begin our

▼ Porta Maggiore

always uphill, we enter Via Ranieri and right again to Via Ripa di Serancia with a fine thirteenth-century *arch* decorated with a ring of dentils and with a small two-light window in pure Romanesque style above. After passing under this stone arch we reach *Piazza San Giovanni* with the church of the same name and a convent with a large and well-known early sixteenth-century **cloister** influenced by San Gallo.

▲ Via Cava

The convent now houses the Enoteca Regionale (wine library), and spaces for exhibitions and meetings.

The complex originated in medieval times and is traditionally believed to have been built over the ancient theater of Costantino Copronico. The church was completely torn down after the earthquake of 1697 and rebuilt shortly afterwards in hexagonal form by the architect Arrigoni with subsequent restorations in classical style on the facade. There are various remains of the original church inside. Behind the altar is a fresco with the *Madonna and Child* attributed to Ugolino di Prete Ilario. The bell tower, dating

▶ The great medieval archway leading to Piazza San Giovanni

▲ Cloister of the former convent of San Giovanni (early 16th cent.)

to 1928, was designed by the architect Branzoni on suggestions furnished by Giovannoni.

Continue your walk along the bastions of Via Ripa Medici to reach *Porta Romana*, built outside the city for Pius VII in 1822. From Porta Romana, Via Garibaldi once more takes us to the center and Piazza della Repubblica.

◄ View of the cliff

SECOND ITINERARY

With Piazza del Duomo once more as our point of departure, along Via Maitani one encounters *Palazzo Fontanieri* (now a hotel) and then on to Piazza Febei with the *Church of San Francesco,* consecrated by Pope Clement IV in 1266. The facade is in tufa with three portals, the central one of which is in marble

▼ The Cathedral seen from Via Maitani

◄ Facade of the church of San Francesco

with a Gothic splay consisting of a sequence of many small elegant columns which move into a pointed arch above the capitals. At the center of the tympanum is a symbolic lamb. The interior has a nave only, transformed into neoclassic Baroque forms with large side chapels. Each one has a large canvas over the altar – by Cesare Nebbia, Filippo Naldini and Hendrick Van den Broeck. The great polychrome wooden crucifix, one of the three of the workshop of Lorenzo Maitani (the "Maestro Sottile") still in Orvieto, hangs over the high altar. At the center of the apse is another large canvas by Naldini with the Vision of Saint Francis. Recently the layer of whitewash has been removed from important fourteenth-century frescoes. They were already mentioned by Perali ("Orvieto", 1919, p.109) and are in an adjacent Gothic chapel with robust cross-rib vaulting. This cycle of frescoes contains the stories of Saint Matthew and is attributed to the Orvieto painter Piero di Puccio known in particular for his documented and famous frescoes in the Camposanto of Pisa, of 1391. The two famous marble statues of *Pope Boniface VIII*, which the City of Orvieto had made in 1297 in his honor to thank him for what he had done for the city, are now on exhibit in the first chapel to the left. Originally they were set in aedicules over Porta Maggiore and Porta Postierla. They were in such poor condition (the head is missing of one of the statues) that it was thought best to house them inside. They recall the art of Arnolfo di Cambio. There is also a fine sixteenth-century cloister, probably by Scalza, in the former Franciscan convent. Along Via Ippolito Scalza on the left, we reach the small church of *San Lorenzo "de arari"* (perhaps from the name of an Etruscan altar which now supports the table of the high altar), in Piazza Santa Chiara. The church, disfigured by time, was restored in an attempt to return it to the original late thirteenth-century Romanesque forms. The simple facade has a portal in Renaissance style with a faded late fifteenth-century fresco in the lunette. The nave is separated from the two aisles by squat cylindrical columns supporting round-headed arches. The high altar is protected by a typical stone ciborium, dating to between the twelfth and thirteenth century, poorly restored in the early 1900s.

▼ Church of San Francesco, detail of the Stories of Saint Matthew attributed to Piero di Puccio (late 14th cent.)

▲▼ Church of San Lorenzo "de Arari" and the apse fresco with Christ Enthroned and Saints (13ᵗʰ cent.)

The most interesting aspect of the decoration is the *pulpit* with Cosmati mosaics and the frescoes dating to the thirteenth, fourteenth, fifteenth centuries which cover the walls and even the columns. The most important one is in the apse conch and depicts *Christ Enthroned and Saints*. It is late thirteenth century, with hints of the art of Cavallini, but it has been repainted so often that interpretation is difficult. The frescoes above on the right of the nave are in better shape. They depict four *stories of Saint Lawrence* and seem to be late thirteenth or early fourteenth-century works.

What can be seen under the repainting on the small panel with the *Madonna* on the altar on the left seems to indicate a fourteenth-century work.

Retracing our steps along Via Scalza, and once more crossing Piazza Febei with the church of San Francesco, along Via Beato Angelico we reach Piazza Ippolito Scalza with the noble *Palazzo Clementini*, known as *Palazzo del Cornelio*. It was indeed commissioned by Monaldo Cornelio Clementini on designs by Scalza in the second half of the sixteenth century. It currently houses the Municipal Library named after Luigi Fumi, expert in local history but rather too unconventional in his attempts to give the city "new-ancient" features.

Continuing along Via Luca Signorelli, Piazza Gualterio, crossing Via del Duomo and turning left to enter Corso Cavour, the main street in Orvieto we immediately encounter the theater, *Teatro Comunale Mancinelli*, and then, still leftwards along Via Felice Cavallotti, to Piazza XXIX Marzo with the *church of San Domenico*. The original thirteenth-century structure as a whole no longer exists, and the imposing nave was torn down to make way for a modest building in Fascist style, at the time a women's academy for physical training now occupied by the Guardia di Finanza. This disgraceful mutilation dates to 1934, with orders received from ....above! The same thing

▼ Palazzo Clementini known as Cornelio designed by Ippolito Scalza

Child. The interior has lost its fresco decorations except for a few dating to the fourteenth century and a wooden Crucifix of the same date. There are also the wooden remains of what tradition says was the Chair from which Saint Thomas Aquinas preached.

The most important work in San Domenico is without doubt the incomplete **Tomb of Cardinal Guglielmo De Braye**, who died in 1282. This outstanding example of thirteenth-century

happened to the adjacent Dominican convent. All that is left of this imposing architectural complex is the transept and the apse of the church. A new pseudo-Gothic facade was grafted onto the left end of the transept, with a Gothic portal moved here from the church of the Armeni in località Tamburino. There is a fine late Gothic fresco in the lunette with the Madonna and

▶ Church of San Domenico, Orvieto painter, Madonna and Child, fresco in the lunette (late 14th/early 15th cent.)

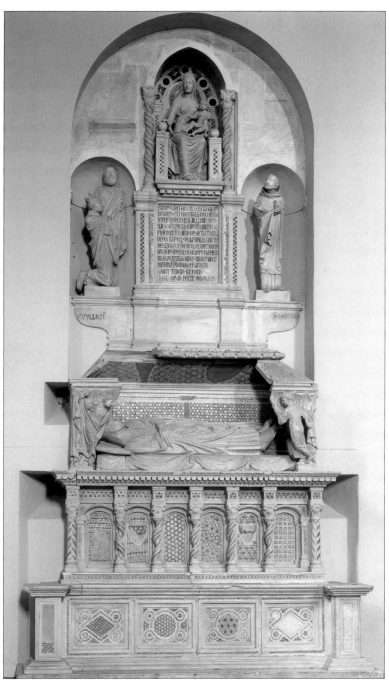

▲ Church of San Domenico, Arnolfo di Cambio,
funeral monument for Cardinal Guglielmo De Braye

Italian art in marble (1285) was signed by Arnolfo di Cambio. Unfortunately once more the hand of man has done more damage here than time. The monument was repeatedly dismantled and moved and a new final attempt at recomposing it is now being made by reinserting fragments in the Museo dell'Opera. Although the monument must have originally been covered by a Gothic

▼ Church of San Domenico,
Michele Sanmicheli,
Petrucci funeral chapel

baldachin with arcading, it will now be set against the wall. Even so the work still glitters with mosaics in the style of the Cosmati masters (Pietro di Oderisio?). In the central portion, supported by twisted columns alternating with mosaic panels in polychrome marble, two lovely angels are drawing back the curtains of the baldachin to reveal the reclining figure of the cardinal. Further up Saint Dominic and Saint William are presenting the cardinal to the Virgin and Child, sitting on a throne with a long dedicatory inscription below.

Around 1513-1517 Michele Sanmicheli built a stupendous funerary *Chapel* for the *Petrucci* family under the apse of the church, as a sort of crypt. It is octagonal in form, with a square "apse" (*scarsella*). This pure Renaissance structure betrays a knowledge of Bramanti's style, but Sanmichele handled it in his own uniquely personal and elegant way.

Back on Corso Cavour we can stop at the charming Romanesque *church of Santo Stefano*, with its fourteenth-century frescoes, or continue along Via Arnolfo di Cambio, Piazza Angelo da Orvieto, Via Roma where about half way up, we turn into Via Belisario to reach the *church of Santa Maria dei*

▲ Facade of the small Romanesque church of Santo Stefano

Servi which once housed the large Maestà formerly attributed to Coppo di Marcovaldo and now in the Museo dell'-Opera. Once more, the result of human neglect, the old Romanesque Gothic thirteenth-century church, in ruins, was totally transformed after the middle of the nineteenth century by Virgilio Vespignani with a white neoclassic facade with six tall pilasters with Corinthian capitals, two lateral niches and a triangular tympanum. Inside is a fine detached late fourteenth-century fresco of the *Madonna Enthroned and Child* and a fine marble *holy water font* dating to the sixteenth century.

At this point we have reached the eastern end of the cliff. Here Cardinal Egidio Albornoz, in the service of the Church of Rome, had an imposing fortress begun in 1364, called *Fortezza Albornoz* in his honor. This highly efficient structure for attack and defense was restored in the fifteenth century but left to fall into ruin in the following centuries when it no longer served its purpose. The interior is now a public park, and the lovely **Porta Postierla** or Porta della Rocca, is set next to the bastions with two large high openings terminating in pointed arches in late thirteenth-century Gothic style.

▼ The Fortezza Albornoz: an entrance gate

The city gate therefore antedates the fortress. The splendid view from the top is unmatched anywhere. Near the park is the famous POZZO DI SAN PATRIZIO or Saint Patrick's Well, famous throughout the world. The name seems to derive from a grotto in Ireland where the saint used to withdraw to pray. For everyone now this deep well is synonymous with something that is practically bottomless, with reference in particular to those who throw their endless riches to the wind. Pope Clement VII dei Medici had the well begun in 1529 to ensure the city with a supply of water. It was designed

▼ Porta Postierla (or della Rocca)

▲▼ Saint Patrick's Well

by Antonio da Sangallo the Younger. A great cylinder 62 meters deep is circled by two spiral staircases of 248 steps each, one for the descent, the other for the ascent so that people and beasts of burden coming to get water from the spring at the bottom would not get in each other's way. The inner core is pierced by large windows which provide light for the staircases.

Next to Saint Pa-

▼ Museo Archeologico Claudio Faina, polychrome terra cotta figure in a chlamys (late 5th cent. B.C.), from the Temple of Belvedere

▲ Ruins of the Temple of Belvedere

trick's Well are the remains of an Etruscan temple known as the *Temple of Belvedere*. The numerous architectural terracottas including *antefixes* are in the archaeological museums of Orvieto.

We can reach Piazza del Duomo along *Via Postierla,* passing through *Piazza Marconi* where at n. 11 is the fine *Palazzo Crispo Marsciano*, built in the mid 1600s on a design by Antonio da Sangallo for Tiberio Crispo, illegitimate son of Pope Paul III Farnese. From the square a view of the apse of the cathedral, with the great stained-glass window by Bonino of Assisi.

A silent city underground
Archaeological itineraries

Orvieto also has a sort of spell-binding underground city dug into the tufa that lies beneath the historical center. The Etruscans were the first to begin digging cisterns for rainwater and other useful spaces in the rock. Excavation continued apace in the Middle Ages and large cavities were dug out to provide families with cellars and storage as well as working spaces. Over 1200 cavities have so far been surveyed, all man-made, some quarries for pozzolana, used for

▲ The "Grotte del Funaro" where ropes were once made

making cement, and some for kilns where the famous painted glazed Orvieto pottery was made. Pottery remains, now rare and almost priceless, have also been

◄ Cave used as a wine cellar (Cantine Foresi)

ound in dump shafts (*pozzi di butto*) where broken or imperfect pieces were thrown.

Two itineraries make it possible for the visitor to tour some of the most interesting of these caves. One is known as the *Archaeological itinerary of Pozzo della Cava*, named after its major attraction, a sixteenth-century well with spring water 32 meters deep, and with traces of a small Etruscan shaft on one side. Entrance is from Via della Cava every day, except Monday, from 8 A.M. to 8 P.M. Entrance fee.

The second itinerary, *Orvieto Underground,* provides a tour of various caves, many quite spacious, used as wine cellars, an oil mill, quarries, with cisterns and well shafts. Others reached via a flight of steps and galleries have rooms with tubs and grottos which open onto the valley and provide panoramic views. They are the so-called columbaria and the countless small niches (about cm 30x30x30) on the walls were used in raising pigeons which provided food, especially during a siege. Departure is every day from the Tourist Office in Piazza del Duomo, at 11 and 12:15 and afternoons at 4 and 5:15. Guided tour (also in English) and entrance fee.

▼ The old columbaria

▼ Old cave, once used as an oil mill

The Etruscan necropoli

Orvieto and its surroundings was the land of the Etruscans. The life and art of this great civilization has reached us through countless objects of all kinds brought to light in archaeological exploration of the necropoli. In the eighteenth and in the nineteenth century, excavations were not yet scientifically carried out and much information was lost. The buildings and temples of the large and small Etruscan towns have disappeared with the passage of time and with the superposition of new buildings on the old, particularly the new Christian churches. The same applies to the Roman civilization. The foundations including the podium and the staircase are all that remain of the *Temple of Belvedere*, previously mentioned. The necropoli all lie at the base of the cliff. Many hundreds of finds, sometimes of great historical and artistic importance, have been unearthed here and help archaeologists form at least an idea of Etruscan history and art: weapons, shields, cippi, statues, etc. Of particular importance are the examples of Etruscan and Greek pottery, especially the fine Corinthian and black- and red-figure Attic vases. While much of this material is in the local archaeological museums, many pieces are in other Italian and foreign museums.

◄ Etruscan tombs in the Necropolis of Crocifisso del tufo

The most important Etruscan necropolis in Orvieto, both for the finds and for its size, is that known as the **Necropolis of Crocifisso del tufo** (8th-3rd century B.C.). The name comes from a sixteenth-century cross carved in the tufa cliff wall near the necropolis. Located at the base of the cliff of Orvieto, it is near the Umbro-Casentinese state highway, with the apse of the former church of Sant'Agostino right up above on the edge of the cliff.

▲ Necropolis of Crocifisso del tufo, architrave of a tomb incised with the family name

The necropolis consists of dozens of single or double chamber tombs, built in dry masonry of carefully shaped tufa blocks, with a pseudo-vault of rows of projecting blocks. The entrances to the tombs lie along carefully laid out streets which make the whole complex look like a real city. Smaller streets lead off a main street and the tombs are located in "lots" owned by various families.

The name of the deceased or the family is almost always incised in the architrave over the entrance, similar to family chapels in our modern cemeteries.

The necropolis is open every day from 9 A.M. to 7 P.M.

Of particular importance also is the *Necropolis of Cannicella* on the southern slopes of the cliff, a complex which included a sanctuary as well as tombs. Other rock-cut tombs were discovered in the locality known as *Sette Camini*, about 6 kilometers distant from Orvieto. They were decorated with painting, now in the Museo Archeologico Nazionale (the Golini Tombs). The *Hescanas Tombs*, named after the Hescanas family, are also nearby and remains of paintings are still visible on the tomb walls.

Environs
L'Abbazia dei Santi Severo e Martirio

The abbey is located about 3 kilometers from Orvieto, starting at Porta Romana. As you approach you are struck by the fine twelve-sided Romanesque bell tower, similar to the one of the church of Sant'Andrea which however

▼ Panoramic view of the Abbey (Abbazia dei Santi Severo e Martirio)

has been rebuilt in great part. Most of the abbey tower is still original.

The Badia is composed of a complex of buildings which in their monumentality continue to be a point of departure for the study of Medieval architecture. We first hear about it in the twelfth century when it was begun by Benedictine monks, perhaps on an earlier sixth-seventh century nucleus. In 1226 Pope Honorius III passed it to the French Premonstratensian monks of the order of Saint Norbert after the Benedictines had been sent

▼ The bell tower and the ruins of the chapter hall

▲ Maestro dell'Abbazia, Crucifixion and Saints (second half of the 13th cent.)

away in 1221 because they refused to obey the bishop of Orvieto. The Premonstratensians enlarged the abbey with buildings in French style such as the refectory, the chapter hall, etc. In the fifteenth century it was the summer residence of nobles and priests of the curia. Then it declined and fell into ruin. The entire chapter hall disappeared, leaving only one great arch which now frames a marvelous view of the cliff of Orvieto. One still falls under the spell of this stone monument when entering the half-ruined atrium next to the bell tower and the lovely cloister. The abbey then became state property and was remarkably well restored. It now houses a private luxury hotel restaurant.

But the abbey is also known, particularly to art historians, for some of its frescoes, among the most significant of Umbrian thirteenth-century painting. In the old refectory, in a fairly good state, is an imposing *Crucifixion with Saints* attributed to an Orvieto artist active between 1250-70 and known as the "Maestro dell'Abbazia dei Santi Severo e Martirio". The other

▲ Orvieto master, Annunciation (14th cent.)

smaller *Crucifixion* in the apse of the choir of the old twelfth-thirteenth century church is also attributed to him. The small apse projects up high on the eastern end of the church, above the portal of the church in front of which is a portico with a massive round arch, with elegant splay in pure Romanesque style. The interior has a nave only with a fine stone floor in marble tesserae and a mosaic in geometric designs in the Cosmati style.

In the adjacent Oratory, another fresco of the *Madonna, Child and Saints Augustine and Severus* is attributed to the so-called "Master of the Madonna of San Brizio" after the panel in the Signorelli chapel in the cathedral and the frescoes in the church of San Giovenale, previously mentioned[5].

In the same oratory there are also interesting fourteenth-century frescoes including a fine *Annunciation* by an artist whose style recalls that of Pietro Lorenzetti and Sienese painting.

(5) For these important frescoes, see the study by Fratini, indicated in note 4.

Vineyards, medieval hamlets and castles

Mention must of course also be made of one of the most typical agricultural products: the wine of Orvieto, known throughout the world. Fine grapes ripen in the surrounding hills and produce a wine with a characteristic aroma, specifically recognized as a D.O.C. wine (denominazione

▲▼ The Umbrian countryside and its vineyards

origine controllata o premium wine).

The vineyards are now parts of modern farms, with a scattering of medieval hamlets, old fortresses and towered castles which, for centuries, witnessed the bitter wars between the local lords: Castel Viscardo, Allerona, Alviano, Castel Rubello, Prodo, Castelgiorgio, Montecchio, Ficulle, Parrano, Fabro... green land of Umbria!

▲ Alviano, the castle

◄ Castel Viscardo,
castle of the Monaldeschi della Cervara

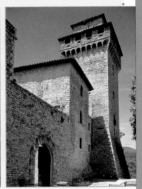

▲ Montecchio, the castle   ▲ Porano, Castel Rubello   ▲ Prodo, the castle

▲ Allerona, gate of the old castle-hamlet

◄ Ficulle, the castle tower
incorporated in the hamlet itself

Useful information

TAKE NOTE

The addresses and information listed below have been chosen at random by the publisher. This has no bearing whatsoever on the quality of whoever or whatever has not been included in this selected list.

HOW TO GET THERE

BY CAR: Toll highway A1 Firenze-Roma – exits Orvieto or Fabro;
From Perugia – super highway (E45) to Todi and S.S. 448 Todi-Orvieto
BY BUS: From and to Rome (Railroad station Tiburtina)
BY TRAIN: Rail line Florence-Rome – Stations of Orvieto or Fabro
BY PLANE: Regional Umbrian airport of Sant'Egidio (Perugia) 90 km. from Orvieto; International airport Leonardo da Vinci (Rome) 130 km. from Orvieto

USEFUL NUMBERS

APT - SERVIZIO TURISTICO TERRITORIALE IAT DELL'ORVIETANO
TOURIST INFORMATION
Piazza Duomo, 24 ☎ 0763 341772
0763 341911 - 0763 343658
🖷 0763 344433
e-mail: info@iat.orvieto.tr.it
www.comune.orvieto.tr.it
www.umbria2000.it
call centre umbria 2000: 848883355
Information office
☎ 0763 341772 🖷 0763 344433
Town Hall - Via Garibaldi ☎ 0763 3061
Taxi - Piazza Matteotti Orvieto Scalo
☎ 0763 301903
Money exchange - Multiservice
Via Largo Barzini, 7 ☎ 🖷 0763 342297
Post office - Via Largo M. Ravelli
☎ 0763 340914
Municipal police
Piazza della Repubblica ☎ 0763 340088

Police precinct
Piazza Cahen ☎ 0763 39211
General emergency (equivalent U.S. 911) 113
Carabinieri Headquarters
Piazza Angelo da Orvieto, 6
☎ 0763 341955-341884 - Emergency 112
Fire Department - Via Monte Subasio
Orvieto Scalo ☎ 0763 302066-305167
Emergency 115
Auto road service ACI
Via Monte Vettore Orvieto Scalo
☎ 0763 305716 - notte 0335 8333631
Emergency 116
Hospital - Loc. Ciconia ☎ 0763 3071
Health emergency ☎ 118
Nights and holidays: doctor on call
☎ 0763 301884
Italian Red Cross - Piazza Duomo, 28
☎ 0763 341727

MONUMENTS

Cathedral - Piazza Duomo
Sacristy ☎ 0763 341167
San Brizio Chapel - Cathedral
Informazioni c/o Opera del Duomo
Piazza Duomo, 26 ☎ 0763 342477
🖷 0763 340336 - e-mail: opsmorv@tin.it
Museo dell'Opera del Duomo
Piazza Duomo - Palazzo Soliano
☎ 0763 342477 🖷 0763 340336
"C. Faina" and Municipal Archaeological Museums
Piazza Duomo, 29 - Palazzo Faina
☎ 0763 341511 🖷 0763 341250
e-mail: fainaorv@tin.it
www.systemnet.it/museo-faina
National Archaeological Museum
Piazza Duomo - Palazzo Papale
☎ 🖷 0763 341039
"Emilio Greco" Museum
Piazza Duomo - Palazzo Soliano
☎ 0763 344605 🖷 0763 344664
Pozzo di San Patrizio (St. Patrick's Well)
Viale Sangallo
☎ 0763 343768 🖷 0763 344664

Torre del Moro - Corso Cavour
☎ 0763 344567
Etruscan necropolis - S.S. 71 al Km. 1,6
☎ 0763 343611
Orvieto Underground "Parco delle Grotte"
☎ 0763 344891 - 0339 7332764
🖷 0763 391121
e-mail: speleotecnica@libero.it
Pozzo della Cava - Via della Cava, 28
☎ 0763 342373 🖷 0763 341029
e-mail: info@pozzodellacava.it

HOTELS

ORVIETO HISTORICAL CENTER

**** Aquila Bianca - Via Garibaldi, 13
☎ 0763 341246 🖷 0763 342273
www.argoweb.it/hotel_aquilabianca/
**** Maitani - Via Lorenzo Maitani, 5
☎ 0763 342011/2/3 🖷 0763 342011
www.argoweb.it/hotel_maitani/
**** Palazzo Piccolomini
Piazza Ranieri, 36
☎ 0763 341743 🖷 0763 391046
e-mail: piccolomini.hotel@orvienet.it
www.argoweb.it/hotel_piccolomini/
*** Corso - Corso Cavour, 343
☎ 🖷 0763 342020
e-mail: hotelcorso@libero.it
*** Duomo - Vicolo di Maurizio, 7
☎ 0763 341887 🖷 0763 341105
www.argoweb.it/hotel_duomo/
*** Filippeschi - Via Filippeschi, 19
☎ 🖷 0763 343275
www.argoweb.it/hotel_filippeschi/
*** Grand Hotel Italia
Via di Piazza del Popolo, 13
☎ 0763 342065/6 🖷 0763 342902
e-mail: hotelita@libero.it
www.argoweb.it/hotel_italia/
*** Grand Hotel Reale
Piazza del Popolo, 27
☎ 🖷 0763 341247
*** Valentino - Via Angelo da Orvieto, 32
☎ 🖷 0763 342464
e-mail: valentino@orvienet.it
www.argoweb.it/hotel_valentino/
*** Virgilio - Piazza Duomo, 5
☎ 0763 341882 🖷 0763 343797

** Posta - Via Luca Signorelli, 18
☎ 🖷 0763 341909
* Virgilio Dipendenza - Via delle Scalette, 2
☎ 0763 341882 🖷 0763 343797

ORVIETO SCALO AND ENVIRONS

**** La Badia - Loc. La Badia, 8
☎ 0763 301959-301876
🖷 0763 305396
e-mail: labadia.hote@tiscalinet.it
**** Villa Ciconia - Via dei Tigli, 69
☎ 0763 305582 🖷 0763 302077
www.argoweb.it/hotel_villaciconia/
*** Europa - Via Antonio Gramsci, 5
☎ 0763 302171/2/3 🖷 0763 305227
e-mail: hoteleuropa@libero.it
www.argoweb.it/hotel_europa/
*** Gialletti - Via Angelo Costanzi, 71
☎ 0763 301981 🖷 0763 305064
www.paginegialle.it/gialletti/
*** Kristall - Via Angelo Costanzi, 69
☎ 0763 302103 🖷 0763 302765
e-mail: kristall@orvienet.it
www.argoweb.it/hotel_kristall/
*** Orvieto - Via Angelo Costanzi, 65
☎ 0763 302751/2 🖷 0763 302753
e-mail: ago@orvienet.it
*** Villa Acquafredda
Loc. Acquafredda, 1
☎ 0763 393073 🖷 0763 390226
www.argoweb.it/hotel_villacquafredda/
** Etruria - Via Angelo Costanzi, 104
☎ 0763 301807 🖷 0763 300535
e-mail: hoteletruria@tiscalinet.it
www.argoweb.it/hotel_etruria/
** Paradiso - Via Sette Martiri, 49
☎ 0763 301894 🖷 0763 390142
** Pergoletta - Via Sette Martiri, 5
☎ 🖷 0763 301418
** Picchio - Via G. Salvatori, 17
☎ 0763 301144-301846
🖷 0763 301144
e-mail: danieletes@libero.it
www.argoweb.it/hotel_picchio/
** Umbria - Via Monte Nibbio, 1
☎ 0763 301940 🖷 0763 305646
www.argoweb.it/hotel_umbria/
* Centrale - Via Sette Martiri, 68
☎ 0763 305881

Country residences

Lineaverde - Via della Stazione, 58
Baschi ☎ 🖷 0744 957685
Paola - Lago di Corbara S.S. 448 - Baschi
☎ 0744 950536 🖷 0744 950186
Xapa - Via della Chiesa, 2
Fraz. Acqualoreto - Baschi
☎ 🖷 0744 958151
La Città del Sole - Fraz. San Vito in Monte
Voc. Casavecchia - San Venanzo
☎ 075 8708206 🖷 075 8708235
cittadelsol@hotmail.com
www.la_città_del_sole.com

Farm holiday centers around Orvieto

Orvieto

La Cacciata - Loc. la Cacciata, 6
☎ 0763 305481
☎ 🖷 0763 300892-341373
www.argoweb.it/agriturismo_cacciata/
San Giorgio - Loc. San Giorgio, 6
☎ 🖷 0763 305221
www.argoweb.it/agriturismo_sangiorgio/
Selva di Osarella - Loc. Osarella, 53
☎ 🖷 0763 302671
Sossogna - Loc. Rocca Ripesena, 61
☎ 🖷 0763 343141
Locanda Rosati - Loc. Buon Viaggio, 22
☎ 🖷 0763 217314
www.locandarosati.orvieto.tr.it
Podere Casale - Loc. Benano, 65/b
☎ 🖷 0763 361001
www.argoweb.it/agriturismo_poderecasale/
Pomonte - Loc. Canino, 1
☎ 🖷 0763 304080
e-mail: pomonte@orvienet.it
www.pomonte.it
Tenuta di Corbara - Loc. Corbara, 7
☎ 0763 304003 🖷 0763 304152
Tenuta di Torricella - Loc. Corbara, 41
☎ 0763 304003 🖷 0763 304152
Tordimaro - Loc. Tordimonte, 37
☎ 0763 304227 🖷 0763 304085
e-mail: tordimaro@tiscalinet.it
Borgo S. Faustino - Loc. S. Faustino, 11/12
☎ 0763 215303 🖷 0763 215745

L'Elmo - Loc. S. Faustino, 18
☎ 0763 215219 🖷 0763 215790
e-mail: lelmo@tiscalinet.it
www.umbriagritour.com
Titignano - Loc. Titignano
☎ 0763 308000/22 🖷 0763 308002

Environs of Orvieto (9-30 km)

L'Uva e le Stelle - Loc. Boccetta III, 9
Porano ☎ 0763 374781 🖷 0763 375923
e-mail: info@uvaelestelle.com
www.uvaelestelle.com
Pomurlo Vecchio - Loc. Pomurlo Vecchio
Baschi ☎ 0744 950190 🖷 0744 950500
e-mail: pomurlovecchio@tiscalinet.it
www.argoweb.it/agriturismo_pomurlovecchio
Le Casette - Loc. Le Casette - Montecchio
☎ 0744 957645-950190 🖷 0744 950500
e-mail: pomurlovecchio@tiscalinet.it
www.argoweb.it/agriturismo_pomurlovecchio
Barberani - Loc. Cerreto - Baschi
☎ 0763 341820 🖷 0763 340773
e-mail: agriturismo@barberani.it
www.barberani.it
Il Casanova - Loc. Cerreto - Civitella del Lago
☎ 0744 950368-950135 🖷 0744 950383
www.argoweb.it/agriturismo_casanova/
Le Macchie - Loc. Pianatonda, 143
Baschi ☎ 0338 7472075 - 0339 2977632
🖷 0763 302639
e-mail: ade.tozzi@tiscalinet.it
Lo Scoglio - Loc. Carnaro - Montecchio
☎ 🖷 0744 951072
e-mail: elgagili@tiscalinet.it
www.agriturismoloscoglio.it
Poggio della Volara
Via San Savino, 32 - Montecchio
☎ 🖷 0744 951820 - 0347 3352523
Le Crite - Loc. Le Crite - Civitella del Lago
☎ 02 76014327 🖷 02 76014354
Palombara - Loc. Palombara, 91
Allerona ☎ 0763 831108
Selvella - Loc. Selvella, 5 - Allerona
☎ 0763 628346 🖷 0763 628166
www.argoweb.it/agriturismo_selvella/
La Casella - Loc. La Casella - Ficulle
☎ 0763 86684-86588 🖷 0763 86684
e-mail: lacasella@tin.it
www.lacasella.com

Poggio Miravalle - Loc. Cornieto, 2
Monteleone d'Orvieto ☎ ⌨ 0763 835309
Belvedere - Loc. Pornello - San Venanzo
☎ ⌨ 075 875411
Borgo Poggiolo - Str. Prov.le 57
Pornellese, km. 6,8 - Loc. Pornello
San Venanzo ☎ 075 8709229-875417
⌨ 075 8709229
e-mail: borgo.poggiolo@tiscalinet.it
www.borgopoggiolo.com
San Pietro Acquaeortus - Loc. Leprara, 24
Allerona ☎ 0763 628130 ⌨ 0763 628008
e-mail: booking@sanpietroweb.it

Religious institutions offering hospitality

Istituto SS. Salvatore - Via del Popolo, 1
☎ ⌨ 0763 342910
www.argoweb.it/istituto_sansalvatore/
Villa Mercede - Via Soliana, 2
☎ 0763 341766 ⌨ 0763 340119
**Casa di Accoglienza Religiosa
San Lodovico** - Piazza Ranieri, 5
☎ 0763 342255 ⌨ 0763 391380
e-mail: s.lodovico@orvienet.it
Convento S. Crispino da Viterbo
Loc. Cappuccini, 8 ☎ 0763 341387

Holiday houses

Casa per Ferie S. Paolo - Via Postierla, 20
☎ 0763 340579 ⌨ 0763 343978
e-mail: cscorvieto@tiscalinet.it

Youth hostel

Porziuncola - Loc. Cappuccini, 8
☎ 0763 341387

Houses and apartments for vacations

Orvieto

Relay Country Marchesa Nerina
Loc. Tignano, 7 ☎ ⌨ 0763 308022
Casa Vacanza Boriano - Le Macchie, 15
Fraz. Canale ☎ 0763 29008/075 35614
⌨ 075 35614

Environs of Orvieto (9-30 km)

Acquaviva - Voc. Acquaviva - Allerona
☎ 0763 628130/0368 7284271
⌨ 0763 628008
e-mail: booking@sanpietroweb.it
Azienda Agraria Poggiovalle
Loc. Poggiovalle - Fabro
☎ 075 9234/0578 248125
⌨ 0578 248219 www.poggiovalle.com
e-mail: inf@poggiovalle.com
Borgo Santa Maria
Loc. Vicinnove - Monteleone
☎ 0348 5167321 ⌨ 0573 832479
e-mail: bsantamaria@tiscalinet.it
web.tiscalinet.it/borgosantamaria
Vecchio Frantoio - Via Botanica
Loc. Fosso Colonna - Monteleone
☎ 0338 3053380 ⌨ 0763 832412
Casaglia Vacanze - Voc. Casaglia, 6
Fraz. San Vito in Monte - San Venanzo
☎ 075 5007386-833113
⌨ 075 8359350
Il Colle - Voc. Ciciano, 36
Fraz. Civitella dei Conti - San Venanzo
☎ 075 8748567/0360 969119
L'Aquilone - Fraz. Poggio Aquilone
San Venanzo ☎ ⌨ 075 8743512
La Torre di Pornello - Loc. Pornello
Voc. La Torre, 32 - San Venanzo
☎ 075 875268/0335 6576896
⌨ 075 875268
Villa Spante - Fraz. Ospedaletto
San Venanzo ☎ 075 8709134-8709272
⌨ 075 8709201

Room rentals

Orvieto

Alle scalette del Duomo
Via dei Gualtieri, 34 ☎ 0338 1853570
D'Annunzio Fuschino Maria
Via dei Lattanzi, 23 ☎ 0763 341079
Patrignani Ricci Fiora - Via dell'Olmo, 1
☎ 0763 341083
Sant'Angelo - Corso Cavour, 152
☎ 0763 343607
Valentina - Piazza Duomo, 2
☎ ⌨ 0763 341611
e-mail: valentina.z@tiscalinet.it

Orvieto Scalo and Environs

Caprasecca Valerio - Viale I Maggio, 43
☎ 0763 301950 🖨 0763 390040
Il Riposino - Loc. San Martino, 16
☎ 0763 390070 🖨 0763 390156
e-mail: sam@tokunga.co.jp
Miki Affittacamere
Piazza della Chiesa, 14 - Fraz. Sugano
☎ 0763 217115
Testaguzza Alessandra
Loc. La Svolta, 36/a
☎ 0763 301846 🖨 0763 301144
e-mail: danieletes@libero.it
www.argoweb.it/hotel_picchio/

Camp grounds

Scacco Matto
Lago di Corbara - S.S. 448 - Baschi
☎ 0744 950163 🖨 0744 950373
Il Falcone - Loc. Vallonganino
Civitella del Lago - Baschi
☎ 🖨 0744 950249
e-mail: ilfalcone@tin.it
www.paginegialle.it/ilfalcone
Agricampeggio Sossogna
Rocca Ripesena, 61- Orvieto
☎ 🖨 0763 343141
Agricampeggio Erbadoro
Fraz. S. Maria Monteleone
☎ 🖨 0763 835241

Wine libraries (Enoteca)

Enoteca Regionale - Piazza S. Giovanni, 1
☎ 0763 394504 🖨 0763 393342
e-mail: itinera.orvieto@tiscalinet.it
La Loggia - Via Loggia dei Mercanti, 6
☎ 0763 344371
e-mail: elaloggia@tin.it
Foresi - Piazza Duomo, 2
☎ 🖨 0763 341611 e-mail: itforesi@tin.it
www.argoweb.it/cantina_foresi/
Orvieto terra d'Umbria
Via Duomo, 23 ☎ 🖨 0763 343074
Tozzi - Piazza Duomo, 13
☎ 0763 344393
Tuttifrutti - Corso Cavour, 146
☎ 0763 344816

Where to eat

Orvieto historical center

Ai Vecchi Sapori - Via Magalotti, 22-24
☎ 0763 342661
Al Pozzo Etrusco - Piazza de' Ranieri, 1/a
☎ 🖨 0763 344456
Al San Francesco - Via B. Cerretti, 10
☎ 0763 343302 🖨 0763 340283
Antico Bucchero - Via de' Cartari, 4
☎ 0763 341725 🖨 0763 391597
Buca di Bacco - Corso Cavour, 299/301
☎ 🖨 0763 344792
Cucina del Grillo
Piazza Angelo da Orvieto, 7
☎ 0763 340972 🖨 0763 344827
Dell'Ancora
Via di Piazza del Popolo, 7-9-11
☎ 0763 342766 🖨 0763 344455
Del Cocco - Via Garibaldi, 4-6
☎ 🖨 0763 342319
Dell'Orso - Via della Misericordia, 16-18
☎ 0763 341642
Del Moro - Via San Leonardo, 7
☎ 🖨 0763 342763
Duca di Orvieto - Via della Pace, 5
☎ 🖨 0763 344663
Il Giglio d'oro - Piazza Duomo, 8
☎ 0763 341903
Il Labirinto - Via della Pace, 26-36
☎ 🖨 0763 342527
I Sette Consoli - Piazza S. Angelo, 1/a
☎ 🖨 0763 343911
La Bottega del Buon Vino
Via della Cava, 26
☎ 0763 342373 🖨 0763 341029
La Grotta - Via Luca Signorelli, 5
☎ 🖨 0763 341348
La Locanda dei Barbetti
Corso Cavour, 312
☎ 0763 340873 🖨 0763 340874
L'Asino d'Oro - Vicolo del Popolo, 9
☎ 0763 344406
La Palma - Corso Cavour, 326
☎ 0763 340840 🖨 0763 341145
La Palomba - Via Cipriano Manente, 16
☎ 🖨 0763 343395
La Pergola - Via dei Magoni, 9/b
☎ 0763 343065

L'Alfiere Verde - Piazza del Popolo, 2-3
☎ 0763 343463 🖷 0763 300166
L'Antica Rupe - Vicolo Sant'Antonio, 2/a
☎ 🖷 0763 343063
La Taverna dell'Etrusco
Via della Misericordia, 5
☎ 0763 343947
La Taverna de' Mercanti
Via Loggia dei Mercanti, 34
☎ 0763 393327 🖷 0763 342898
La Volpe e l'Uva - Via Ripa Corsica, 1
☎ 🖷 0763 341612
Le Grotte del Funaro
Via Ripa Serancia, 41
☎ 0763 343276 🖷 0763 342898
Maurizio - Via Duomo, 78
☎ 0763 341114-343212
🖷 0763 344438
Mezza Luna - Via Ripa Serancia, 3
☎ 0763 341234
Peng Cheng - Corso Cavour, 443
☎ 0763 343355
Osteria dell'Angelo
Piazza XXIX Marzo, 8/a
☎ 0763 341805
San Giovenale - Piazza San Giovenale, 6
☎ 0763 340641/2 🖷 0763 343948
Tipica Trattoria Etrusca
Via Lorenzo Maitani, 10
☎ 0763 344016 🖷 0763 341105
Zeppelin - Via Garibaldi, 28
☎ 0763 341447 🖷 0763 305781

Orvieto Scalo and environs

Da Nino - Via Sette Martiri, 45-47
☎ 🖷 0763 300478
Gialletti - Via Angelo Costanzi, 71
☎ 0763 300323 🖷 0763 340283
Girarrosto del Buongustaio
Loc. Tamburino, 81 ☎ 🖷 0763 341935
La Badia - Loc. La Badia, 8
☎ 0763 301876 🖷 0763 301959
La Pergoletta - Via Sette Martiri, 5
☎ 🖷 0763 301901
Le Bighe - Via A. Costanzi, 92-96
☎ 0763 301458 🖷 0763 300525
Biagio - Loc. Biagio, 21 ☎ 0763 28628
Il Portonaccio - Via Angelo Costanzi, 67
☎ 🖷 0763 300022

Ritrovo del Cacciatore
Loc. Villanova, 12
☎ 0763 217107 🖷 0763 344827
I Tre Piccioni - Via G. Falcone, 20
(stadio comunale) ☎ 🖷 0763 305895
Umbria - Via Monte Nibbio, 1/3
☎ 0763 301940-305897
🖷 0763 305646
Villa Ciconia - Via dei Tigli, 69 - Ciconia
☎ 0763 305582/3 🖷 0763 302077
Antica Trattoria Buonrespiro
Loc. Buonrespiro, 26 ☎ 0763 28670
Da Dina - Via Angelo Costanzi, 78-80
☎ 🖷 0763 301842
Da Gregorio - Loc. Morrano, 136/7
☎ 0763 215011
Del Conte - Loc. Buonrespiro, 18
☎ 0763 217046
La Graticola - Via dei Tigli, 11 - Ciconia
☎ 0763 301802
La Mora - Loc. Buonviaggio, 18
☎ 0763 375037/22 🖷 0763 375022
Da Peppe di Canonica
Loc. Canonica, 56 ☎ 0763 217232
Da Valerio - Viale I Maggio, 37-39
☎ 🖷 0763 301950

Pizza and sundry

Orvieto

Pizzeria Bugnini - Corso Cavour, 213
☎ 0763 341859
Pizzeria Capriccio - Via L. Signorelli, 9
☎ 0763 342852
Pizzeria Charlie - Corso Cavour, 194
☎ 0763 344766 🖷 0763 301649
Pizzeria Chiolle Sandra
Piazza del Popolo, 20b ☎ 0763 341587
Pizzeria Al Cordone - Via Filippeschi, 22
☎ 0763 341817
Pizzeria I Dolci di Moscatelli
Corso Cavour, 11 ☎ 0763 341458
Pizzeria Forno del 2000
Corso Cavour, 282 ☎ 0763 341722
Pizzeria Paolieri - Corso Cavour, 49
☎ 0763 342370
Pizzeria San Domenico
Piazza XXIX Marzo, 18 ☎ 0763 344608
Pizzeria Santi - Via Cesare Nebbia, 22

Pizzeria Sosta - Corso Cavour, 100
☎ 0763 343025
Pizzeria Tavern Engel Keller
P.zza Ippolito Scalza, 2 ☎ 0763 341098
Pizzeria 2000 - Corso Cavour, 200
☎ 0347 3013149
Antica Cantina - Piazza Monaldeschi, 18-19
☎ 🖨 0763 344746
Caffè Cavour - Corso Cavour, 74
☎ 0763 342510
Caffè del Corso - Corso Cavour, 158
☎ 0763 344724
Hescanas - Piazza Duomo, 31
☎ 🖨 0763 342578
La Fraschetta - Vicolo del Pozzo Bianco, 2
☎ 0763 343075
La Vecchia Cava - Via della Cava, 83
☎ 0763 342256
Montanucci - Corso Cavour, 21
☎ 0763 341261
Sabatini - Corso Cavour, 326
☎ 0763 342418
Sant'Andrea - Piazza della Repubblica, 25
☎ 0763 343285
Teatro - Piazza Fracassini, 11
☎ 0763 340705
Velzna - Corso Cavour, 111 ☎ 0763 341313

ORVIETO SCALO AND ENVIRONS

Pizzeria Bar Zelletta - Via dei Fiordalisi, 2/4
Ciconia ☎ 0763 305333
Pizzeria del Ponte - Via dei Gelsi, 1
Ciconia ☎ 0763 305477
Pizzeria Due Pini
Fontanelle di Bardano, 31 ☎ 0763 316050
Pizzeria Il Grifone - Via Sette Martiri, 60
☎ 0347 8400260
Pizzeria I Portici - Viale I Maggio, 73
☎ 0763 301414
Pizzeria La Funicolare
Piazza Matteotti, 3/5 ☎ 0763 300092
Pizzeria La Pizza - Viale A. Costanzi, 68
☎ 0763 300321
Pizzeria La Preferita - Viale degli Aceri, 18
Ciconia ☎ 0763 305248
Pizzeria Lo Stornello - Viale Tevere, 32
☎ 0763 393397
Pizzeria Pam Pam - Via degli Ulivi, 11
Ciconia ☎ 0763 302403
Pizzeria Subito Subito - Via Arno, 8
☎ 0763 343197
Pizzeria Verde Luna - Via Adige, 16
☎ 0763 344676
Pizzeria Lord Byron Pub
Piazza del Commercio, 7 ☎ 0763 302164

REPRINT 2004

Publishing manager: Barbara Bonechi
Coordination and revision of texts and iconographical research: Lorena Lazzari
Graphic design and maps: Paola Rufino
Layout: Sabrina Menicacci
Photo credits: Archives of Bonechi Edizioni "Il Turismo", photographers Nicola Grifoni (Florence), Massimo Roncella (Orvieto), Claudio Tini (Caprarola)
Photos on pages 29 (above), from 32 to 42, 44, 61, 62 (above), 64, 65, 66, 67, 68 (above), 70 "permission kindly granted by the Museo dell'Opera del Duomo di Orvieto";
Page 59 "permission kindly granted by the Soprintendenza Archeologica per l'Umbria, Perugia"; Page 99 (Scala Group - Antella, Florence) and pages 112-113 "permission kindly granted by SBAAAS, Perugia"
Translation: Erika Pauli for Comunicare
Photolithography: Studio Leonardo Fotolito srl., Firenze
Printing: Petruzzi Stampa, Città di Castello (PG)
ISBN 88-7204-504-5

* The location of the works given is where they are to be found as this book goes to press.
* Everything possible has been done to ascertain the legitimate owners of illustration rights. In case of involuntary omissions, we will be happy to take care of the rights in question.

Index

Concessionary agent for Lazio (excluding Rome):
Archidee di Claudio Tini
Località Sant'Egidio
01032 Caprarola (VT)
Tel. e Fax +39-0761.647540
E-mail: archi@thunder.it